Innovation in Odds-Beating Schools

Innovation in Odds-Beating Schools

Exemplars for Getting Better at Getting Better

Kristen Campbell Wilcox, Hal A. Lawson, Janet I. Angelis, Francesca Durand, Karen Gregory, Sarah Zuckerman, and Kathryn Schiller

Foreword by Anthony Bryk

ROWMAN & LITTLEFIELD
Lanham • Boulder • New York • London

Published by Rowman & Littlefield
A wholly owned subsidiary of The Rowman & Littlefield Publishing Group, Inc.
4501 Forbes Boulevard, Suite 200, Lanham, Maryland 20706
www.rowman.com

Unit A, Whitacre Mews, 26-34 Stannary Street, London SE11 4AB

British Library Cataloguing in Publication Information Available

Library of Congress Cataloging-in-Publication Data Available

ISBN 978-1-4758-3007-1 (cloth : alk. paper)
ISBN 978-1-4758-3008-8 (pbk. : alk. paper)
ISBN 978-1-4758-3009-5 (electronic)

♾️™ The paper used in this publication meets the minimum requirements of American
National Standard for Information Sciences—Permanence of Paper for Printed Library
Materials, ANSI/NISO Z39.48-1992.

Printed in the United States of America

Contents

Miracle Goals and No Methods

Foreword by Anthony Bryk

Through the dedicated efforts of many educators, our schools have been gradually improving. The problem is that our aspirations for what we want our schools to accomplish are increasing at a much faster rate. Consequently, a chasm has been growing for some time between these rising aspirations and what schools are able to achieve routinely. And this chasm is greatest for our most disadvantaged students and in our most troubled community contexts. This chasm has now formed as one of the great social justice issues for our time.

In response, we have thrown a rapidly increasing number of new ideas at our education systems over the past decade but often without the practical know-how and the necessary expertise to make these ideas really work. We overpromise and then get frustrated about how difficult the work is and how much time it takes to move from what seems like a good idea to effective execution at scale. We become disillusioned about the reform, it fades into the background, and then we just move on to the next new idea. Rarely do we stop to reflect, "Why do these reform outcomes regularly occur?" Our casual postmortems tend to blame the individuals most immediately involved but fail to see how the task and organizational complexity that characterizes contemporary educational systems shapes much of the consequences that do emerge.

It is no wonder that so many educators today are experiencing "initiative fatigue." Edwards Deming, the improvement guru whose ideas have inspired productive change across many different industries and sectors, said about education that we are a field characterized by "miracle goals and no methods." He said that in 1991 as policy leaders touted Goals 2000. His comment proves equally true in looking back now on No Child Left Behind and remains prescient as we now move into an era of the Common Core, twenty-first-century skills, personalization or whatever framing for new standards may come forward in the future.

In truth, we have no realistic means to accomplish the noble aspirations that we hold—whether it is all children reading by grade 3, all children career and college ready, or all new teachers succeeding in teaching all of their students well. Most daunting in this regard is the recognition that we live in an era of rapid change on a global scale and that this has extraordinary implications for our work ahead. Schools exist to prepare the next generation of young people for the adult world they will inhabit. In an epoch of extraordinary technological and societal change, inevitably the aspirations for our educational institutions will also continue to change, and in all likelihood at an increasing rate.

Clearly, we cannot continue to do what we have always done. We have to get better at getting better.

At one level, _Exemplars for Getting Better at Getting Better_ can be read as a synthetic account of a handful of schools that "Beat the Odds." These schools took on the challenges of implementing the Common Core, introducing more rigorous teacher and principal evaluation systems and becoming more systematic in their use of data to improve student learning. Wilcox and colleagues detail in the pages that follow how these schools effectively engaged in these three major reforms to the technical core of teaching and learning. Given the results that emerged in these "beating the odds" schools, one could be inclined to simply exhort other schools and districts to do the same. If these places succeeded why can't you?

But the book proceeds in a very different direction. It takes up Deming's challenge: by what method can we turn our educational aspirations into meaningful accomplishments? Wilcox et al. offer an impressive account of coherent professional action from school boards and the superintendent's office, through central office staff, to principals, teachers, and out to parents and community organizations. District leaders engaged local educators in learning about each of these reforms and created the necessary space and support for educators to iterate and refine how they might best adapt them in their particular school and community contexts. Organizing such efforts entailed seeing the system that created the current unsatisfactory outcomes, drawing on the best of extant research knowledge for key design principles guiding how to move forward, and then engaging in iterative cycles of disciplined inquiry that focus us on learning by doing.

Numerous insights about how schools can "get better at getting better" abound across the pages of this book. I draw out a few here. Leaders in these "beating the odds" schools recognized that engaging teachers in the design and evolution of reform is essential to meaningful change. This reflects a core improvement principle identified by Edwards Deming: those directly engaged in the work are central to its improvement.

Closely related, these leaders recognized that improvement is not a simple command and control exhortation, "just implement the reform as designed." Rather they understood that productive educational change entails a process of adaptive integration. Typically the reforms we seek to enact are, in essence, solution systems, consisting of many elements that must join coherently together. These solution systems must in turn be integrated well into the socially and politically complex systems that are our educational institutions. The essential improvement question is then, "How do I actually get such an intervention to work with my students and under the constraints of my organizational context and local setting?" Addressing this question requires analytic and empirical discipline. Educators must deeply understand the evidence-based principles that undergird the improvement effort. It also means iterative cycles of trying out new practices, analyzing data—attending to both what's working, and what is not—and continuously improving. For the individuals involved, this is akin to a learning journey; in this case, a learning to improve journey. Even if we begin with good ideas and some good artifacts and guidance about how to use them, improvement has an evolutionary character. Effective change is invented as the learning to improve journey proceeds. This is a very different logic than the more mechanical vision of implementation as following some predefined set of steps or rules.

But an important caveat also needs to be recognized. While we might hold common aspirations for every school, a working theory of improvement must also recognize that schools do not all start in the same place. The organizational differences among schools are much more complex than conveyed in the simple statistics we report about test scores, percent minority, and low-income enrollments. In fact, our reliance on these indicators often masks more than they inform. In this regard, it is important to recognize that, while the "beating the odds" schools served diverse student populations, they also started with some key advantages. They had a stable staff including a cadre of improvement leaders. Teachers in these schools felt safe to try new things, to fail sometimes, and to learn by doing. This was in turn made possible by a solid base of relational trust with their students, parents, colleagues and those who hold formal authority over them, including their school principal and central office leaders.

Consequently, a different and nascent form of accountability could emerge—one focused on learning to improve. The three core improvement questions were alive here: What specific problem are we trying to address? What change(s) might we introduce and why? And how will we know if these change(s) are actually an improvement? When these questions become normative within an organization—embedded in the fabric of its daily work—then the institution becomes genuinely accountable for continuously improving its outcomes. We can ask no more of a school than every educator is a learner and everyone is an improver.

Leaders in these schools and districts, while pressing for change, also provided resources to make learning to improve possible, and maintained realistic expectations as to what "good progress" actually looks like. Especially in the early stages of taking on ambitious changes, learning from trial and error is inevitable and this just takes some time. This means being realistic about how fast any reform can move through an organization and also how much change local educators can possibly absorb in any given period of time.

The processes of school improvement are akin to organic growth phenomena. You can only grow as fast as the current capacity of your organization.

The rapid infusion of more resources, adding more people, exhorting louder, and threatening sanctions cannot accelerate improvement beyond this action-time limit. Put simply, the state of a school's current capacities delimit what is possible to achieve in any next given period of time. Clearly, schools that start with weaker social conditions than found in the "beating the odds" schools will take longer to improve.

And at the boundary, this also means being a critical realist. The base social conditions in some schools are very weak.[1] No matter what program may be assigned to them, little is likely to be taken up and engaged well in these contexts. These places are chronically stressed and often unable to function as the kind of learning organization described in this volume.

These lessons have important implications as we move into the new Every Student Succeeds Act (ESSA) reform era of adopting evidence-based interventions. Educators will now be exhorted to implement programs with the "strongest evidence base." It is critical that we be clear as to what this term actually means. Some will surely interpret it as implying programs that have the biggest effects. Not true. Others might interpret "strongest evidence base" as implying the greatest assurance that this program will work for you. Also not true. Rather, the strongest evidence base simply means that we have reliable evidence that it worked somewhere for someone. Or put simply, that the intervention *can* work. This research base however is largely silent on whether it can work specifically in turnaround school contexts and what it might take to actually do so. So the knowledge we need to address improvements where they are most needed largely does not exist.

Unless we heed the lessons of this book, *Innovation in Odds-Beating Schools,* educators will once again confront a promising idea that will often fail in execution. Achieving quality results entails sustained collective efforts where educators engage in systematic iterative inquiries discerning how to "make it work here." And this, in turn, demands that a base of supportive social relationships either preexist or develop coincident with the take up of the intervention. Here too we hear the voice of Edwards Deming. Although he worked primarily on improvements in the industrial sector, he appreciated both the complexity of the work systems he sought to improve and the intrinsically personal-social character of change efforts. Reading the inspiring and informative exemplars presented in this book by Wilcox et al., I became hopeful that we might finally be able to move past Deming's haunting observation that education has "miracle goals and no methods" and toward a new era of "getting better at getting better."

Anthony S. Bryk
Carnegie Foundation for the Advancement of Teaching
Stanford, California
August 2016

NOTE

1. On this point, see the discussion on truly disadvantaged schools in Chapter 6 of *Organizing Schools for Improvement* (Bryk, A. S., Sebring, P. B., Allensworth, E., Luppescu, S., & Easton, J. Q. (2009). Organizing schools for improvement: Lessons from Chicago. Chicago, IL: Chicago University Press).

Preface

The genesis of this book goes back a decade plus when two of the authors (Janet Angelis and Kristen Wilcox) along with then dean of the University at Albany School of Education Susan Phillips saw an invitation to become the New York State affiliate of the national Just for the Kids project as an opportunity. Among its priorities, Just for the Kids sought to urge and support schools to use best practice research to improve student outcomes.

At that time (2004), state assessments were becoming more high stakes for students and schools; we were hopeful that the comparative case study research we would be doing could help make the results of those assessments more useful to educators and policy makers than the raw scores reported by the state.

Our comparative studies would examine processes and practices in schools that served higher percentages of students growing up in poverty and culturally and linguistically diverse students, yet whose students performed better than predicted. We would also examine processes and practices in schools whose students consistently performed at predicted levels. Our goal was to see if we could find differences in processes and practices between the two groups of schools.

We chose to ground our studies in social ecological theory since we recognize that no part of the education system operates in isolation. Each classroom is nested in a school, which is nested in a district, which is nested in the larger community. And each part of this system influences and is influenced by the others. So, although our studies would focus at the school level, we always would also examine classroom and district practices.

While this research design would facilitate identification of unique characteristics of schools correlated with better student outcomes, we also knew that such "best" or "promising" processes and practices were not likely to be the same in all school settings. Thus, we selected our samples to include smaller and larger rural, suburban, and urban schools and eliminated schools with advantages such as higher wealth ratios.

Since 2004 we have conducted seven such studies, looking first at overall performance at the elementary, middle, and high school levels, then zeroing in on specific concerns voiced by various stakeholders in our state (e.g., performance of English language learners and students with disabilities).

Because our goal was always to provide information that other schools could learn from and use, we shared those findings broadly and began working directly with school leadership teams who wanted to use the findings to help shape their own improvement efforts. To inform this work, we drew on the vast school improvement knowledge base and were drawn, in particular, to the developing field of improvement science (Bryk, Sebring, Allensworth, Luppescu, & Easton, 2009; Bryk, Gomez, Grunow, & LaMahieu, 2015).

When New York State shifted its policy agenda and secured a Race to the Top award from the federal government in 2010, State Education Department (SED) officials who had heard of our work asked if we might conduct similar studies using the first results of Common Core assessments to select our sample. As part of its Race to the Top grant, SED was requiring all schools and districts in the state to implement the following three innovations and to do so simultaneously, beginning in the 2013–14 academic year.

1. The Common Core State Standards (CCSS),
2. Annual professional performance reviews (APPR) for teachers and principals, with results based, in part, on student scores on Common Core assessments, and
3. Systems for data-driven instruction (DDI).

Kristen took up this challenge as principal investigator, and as she shares in the acknowledgments, put together a diverse team from the University at Albany's School of Education to identify the sample and do the field research during the spring and fall of 2014–15. The researchers' areas of expertise span curriculum, instruction, educational policy, educational leadership, and social welfare, and we augmented the team with K-12 educators who shared a knowledge base of direct experience in classrooms and school and district offices.

This book shares the findings of that study. It captures and furthers what we have reported to our SED sponsor about what we learned about how odds-beating schools approached implementing the three innovations of the CCSS, APPR, and DDI.

Along the way we have found that each of us has learned—has had to learn—more about areas outside our core expertise. We couldn't help but realize that just as K-12 educators are needing to take on new roles and workforce configurations as a result of new policy mandates, those of us in higher education also need to become better at crossing boundaries to more effectively deal with what our British colleague Alan Dyson (2016) calls the "wicked problem" of school reform—"wicked" because it involves so many sectors and contexts that it cannot be successful using old formulations of standardized, programmatic solutions.

In this book, we bring together what we have learned from schools whose processes and practices have supported students, teachers, specialists, administrators, and their communities as they worked to "get better at getting better" (Bryk et al., 2015) in an environment of rapid innovation. These K-12 colleagues are engaging in redesigning their school systems in accordance with twenty-first-century needs, demands, and opportunities.

We share what we have learned in the hopes that other educators or those who are preparing to become educators can gain some insights. We especially hope that groups of educators will consider and discuss together how our findings might inform the work they do in their particular setting to also get better at getting better.

REFERENCES

Bryk, A. S., Sebring, P. B., Allensworth, E., Luppescu, S., & Easton, J. Q. (2009). *Organizing schools for improvement: Lessons from Chicago.* Chicago, IL: Chicago University Press.

Bryk, A., Gomez, L., Grunow, A., & LeMahieu, P. (2015). *Learning to improve: How America's schools can get better at getting better.* Cambridge, MA: Harvard Education Press.

Dyson, D. A. (2016, April). Challenges faced by schools in the current environment and options for developing the capacity to address these challenges. Symposium conducted by the University at Albany, State University of New York, Albany, NY.

Acknowledgments

The study on which this book is based could not have happened without the support of John King, former Commissioner of Education for the State of New York, as well as Ken Slentz, his Deputy Commissioner. These two leaders sought out two of the authors (Kristen and Janet) based on prior, similar work we had done as Principal Investigator and Project Director, respectively, for a research-to-practice partnership called NYKids, an outgrowth of the NYS affiliate of the national Just for the Kids project.

NYKids, in turn, could not exist without the support of the State of New York and the University at Albany's School of Education, as well as our advisory board, which includes representative of major statewide education associations and the business community.

Designing and implementing the study took the hard work of many of my colleagues in the School of Education, as did the complex endeavor of contracting the study with the State Education Department (SED). For the latter I extend my sincere gratitude to Alison Olin, Sara Anderson, and Penny Ng in the dean's office, as well as to those administrators at SED who reciprocated the cooperation between our organizations.

In addition to contributing to the field work, colleague and coauthor Hal Lawson provided invaluable leadership in weaving many lines of empirical and theoretical research into our design and analysis. Kathryn Schiller lent her instrumental expertise in sample selection and survey design, and Francesca Durand was pivotal in working with Katy and me in survey and other instrument development and serving as the go-to person on every aspect of the study. Hal, Katy, and Francesca also all participated in the time-intensive effort of conducting the field research and data analysis.

Karen Gregory and Sarah Zuckerman both contributed their deep knowledge of K-12 instruction for diverse learners to data collection and assisted with data analyses. All of these chapter authors and coauthors unselfishly offered their expertise, time, and passion to the effort of conducting the study and preparing their contributions for this book, for which I am sincerely grateful.

Two long-term colleagues with whom I have been conducting this kind of research for many years also played key roles in the study and making this book possible. Sharon Wiles ably led the recruitment effort and coordinated the travel schedules for multiple research teams. And coauthor Janet kept her eagle eye on all reports and products that shared our analyses and most importantly pulled together all components of this book in its final form, from coauthoring chapters to editing final proofs.

Once chapters for this book began to take shape and Janet had taken them as far as she could, Tony Bryk offered his time to discuss the findings and provided valuable feedback on early drafts of the manuscript—I extend my deep appreciation for the incisive feedback and intellectual guidance in navigating the application of improvement science in this text. Our editors at Rowman, Tom Koerner and Carlie Wall, also could not have been more helpful in the preparation of the final manuscript.

Last but not least, I am indebted to all my colleagues who assisted in a variety of capacities including data collection and data analysis. Without their assistance we would have nothing much to share. My sincere gratitude to: Linda Baker, Kathy Nickson, Michael Lawson, Shari Keller, Dorothy Porteus, Ben Malczyk, Michelle Bianchi, Fang (Lisa) Yu, Sharon Wiles, Nisa Felicia, Juliana Svistova, Lynn Lisy-Macan, Deb Byrne, Piera Camposeo, John Costello, Heather Kurto, Aaron Leo, Christl Mueller, Gretchen Oliver, and Kemm Wilson.

K.C.W.

Chapter One

Schools as Innovation-Ready Learning Organizations

Kristen Campbell Wilcox, Hal A. Lawson, and Janet Ives Angelis

Rapid changes in society such as those experienced in the early decades of the twenty-first century provide challenges as well as opportunities to educators and others whose work relates to schools. The trends toward more socioeconomically, culturally, and linguistically diverse communities and increased demands for globally competitive workforces with transferable and complex skills and competencies influence every aspect of life.

Although some of these changes are quickly reflected in schools (e.g., increasing numbers of immigrant, multilingual students), educators often lag behind workers in other sectors in how quickly they respond to them, especially in comparison with sectors where market forces necessitate rapid changes to achieve competitive advantage (Porter, 2008).

Such lags are predictable, in part, because schools are carriers of long traditions, dominant belief systems, preferred public policies, and established social practices. While in principle schools are amenable to change because they are made up of people who are able to learn, freighted as they are with history, in their institutionalized form they are remarkably resistant to change (Darling-Hammond, 2010).

The inherited prototype for what a school is and does, based on an industrial model from earlier centuries, tends to be viewed as a common-sense arrangement (Berger & Luckmann, 1967). This arrangement has considerable traction because nearly every person who has completed school has been inculcated in some measure to believe that "school" as they experienced it is structured, operated, and managed the way it should, or at least needs to be.

Educators are particularly likely to entertain such conserving views, together with the preservationist practices and routines they enact in fulfilling their roles within the organizations they were hired to support (Lortie, 1975). This steadfast adherence to the status quo is particularly evident in

1

schools and districts that lack processes and practices to facilitate the journey of vision, mission, and goals to practice across their organizations (Darling-Hammond & Bransford, 2005).

Dramatic and rapid societal changes the likes of which Americans are experiencing today, challenge status quo orientations and institutionalized school arrangements. So do relatively dramatic and rapidly changing federal and state policy innovations that require educators to adapt not only what they are expected to do, but also how. And there is no indication that the pace of change and demands to meet it are likely to slow in the years ahead.

During these turbulent times, American schools have become lightning rods for multiple, public demands and challenges because school designs, operations, and outcomes are consequential for the economy and democratic citizenship. Schools are, in effect, one of the essential fibers that hold the fabric of a diverse society together.

As this fabric is stretched, America's promise of "life, liberty, and the pursuit of happiness" to all of its citizens is at stake. This is especially true when a deep and a wide gap develops between societal needs and student performance and between those who enjoy privileged and culturally and linguistically dominant group status and those who do not.

In the U.S., schools lie at the center of the promise that demography does not equal destiny (Rothstein, 2004). The premise that schools offer equitable opportunities to learn are rooted in this promise (Raffo, 2014), and the importance of this premise and this promise to the fabric of American communities and the nation grows as student diversity and poverty increase.

The primary challenge during such turbulent times is for schools and school systems to adapt to become better fit for purpose, and to do so in a manner that is appropriate in diverse local contexts. This challenge also presents the opportunity to determine

- Which policies, programs, and practices to maintain, which to modify, and which to eliminate;
- What kind of leadership—and from whom—is required to lead innovation implementation;
- What kinds of curricular, instructional, and resource allocation adaptations are needed for innovation implementation;
- What monitoring systems are needed to determine the effectiveness of innovations in reaching desired outcomes; and
- Which organizational features of schools and district offices need to be adjusted and reconfigured to sustain any gains associated with improvement efforts, while paving the way for future innovations.

Such concerns circulate in all schools, but in some, outcomes are unusual and in a very good way.

In those schools—called "outliers" in some circles, "positive deviants" in others, and here called "odds beaters"—students consistently perform beyond expectations. What educators do and how they do it to create better outcomes for their students in these odds-beating schools, especially during periods of rapid innovation implementation, provides some insight into potential pathways for improvement in other school systems and moves us toward a better understanding of schools as innovation-ready learning organizations.

THE PROBLEM(S) AND WHAT
ODDS-BEATERS CAN TEACH US

Society's aspirations for its educational institutions to innovate quickly and strategically outstrip educators' abilities and resources to do so. Many researchers have come to believe that, as in other sectors, it is only when schools and districts become innovation-ready learning organizations that they will be able to meet the challenges (e.g., Bryk, Gomez, Grunow, & LaMahieu, 2015; your authors).

Bridging the gap between current, and likely future, demands for rapid change and the consequent unprecedented number of requirements placed on schools will require leadership for learning (Knapp, Copland, Honig, Plecki, & Portin, 2014)—student, staff, organizational, and policy learning. The work will not be easy and will require new organizational designs, capacity-building structures and processes, and workforce configurations.

Through illustrations drawn from odds-beating schools, this book demonstrates how educators within them have addressed multiple simultaneous innovation implementation demands and with better than predicted results. Overall, the odds-beating schools provide readers with examples of distributed leadership arrangements, pervasive improvement-oriented attitudes, and goal-oriented, learner-centered approaches to curriculum and instruction, all of which are made possible and cemented by trusting relationships and communications. Through these they achieve an "innovation implementation sweet spot."

These several features help to account for the ability of odds-beating schools to exemplify learning organizations as they adapt new innovations fit for purpose and context.

THE ORIGINS OF THIS BOOK

This book stems from a study conducted in New York State, the fourth most populous in the United States and among the most culturally and linguistically diverse in the nation. The intent of the study was to learn more about how three innovations, the implementation of which occurred simultaneously, were experienced in relatively better-performing schools based on student achievement outcomes and in contrast with typically performing schools.

The three innovations studied were the Common Core State Standards (CCSS); new performance evaluation systems for educators (called the Annual Professional Performance Review [APPR]) based, in part, on students' performance on Common Core assessments; and data-driven instruction (DDI). Details about these innovations are discussed in more detail later.

The focus of the study was strategic and intended to glean insight into what individual and organizational characteristics relate to relative innovation implementation success. In alignment with this focus, the study was grounded in a social-ecological framework, which draws attention to the relationships between and among different systems (Brofenbrenner, 1993; Wilcox & Angelis, 2009; 2010; Wilcox, 2013; Wilcox, Lawson, & Angelis, 2015).

The research team determined that schools to be studied would be identified favoring such demographic factors as poverty and diversity in the student population as these characteristics have been highly correlated with achievement gaps (Coleman et. al, 1966; Goldsmith, 2011). After running a number of statistical tests (see Chapter 9 for a detailed explanation of the sampling procedures) eighteen schools, six typical performers (used for comparison purposes) and twelve odds beaters (oversampled to offer more examples of better performance scenarios), were chosen for the study.

The odds beaters serve a higher poverty and more ethnically and linguistically diverse population than the typical performers overall, yet their students achieved significantly better on the CCSS assessments and also shared a history of better performance on assessments given prior to CCSS implementation.

The sample was also purposeful in that it included schools from all of the state's major geographic regions as well as representing its urban, suburban, and rural communities in order to account for differences in district and school resources, workforce configurations, and a number of other organizational characteristics. These schools represent the variety of schools in the state yet are unusual in that they have disrupted the correlation between their demography and student performance outcomes as measured by the state's high stakes assessments.

Given the schools' demographic profiles and their better-than-predicted student outcomes, the research team then sought to compare the odds-beating schools and typical performers by determining: (1) What educators in the odds-beating schools and their districts do differently than their counterparts in typically performing schools/districts; and, perhaps even more importantly, (2) how and even why they do it despite and even because of the need to implement the three innovations (CCSS, APPR, and DDI) rapidly and simultaneously.

Expanding the Frame: Improvement Science Meets Innovation Science

School improvement studies generally attend to unique features of the improvement agendas of individual schools and districts or those of one or more of the national networks for school improvement such as Success for All (Slavin, Madden, Dolan, & Wasik,1996) and Accelerated Schools (Hopfenberg & Levin, 1993). Each of these proposes its own specialized, scripted improvement framework and protocol.

Some studies have expanded to focus not just on schools but on district office-school relations and interactions as well. These highlight the extent to which district- and school-level policies and leadership practices are clear, coherent, aligned, and justifiable (DuFour & Fullan, 2013; Durand, Lawson, Wilcox, & Schiller, 2016; Knapp et al., 2014).

Other studies have examined the extent to which a school's or an entire district's orientation toward, and readiness for, innovation helps to account for decisions to voluntarily adopt and implement new improvement models and strategies (McDonald, Klein, & Riordan, 2009; Weiner, 2009; Wilcox & Angelis, 2009). And a few have begun to look at the extent to which such schools and districts are learning how to become learning organizations (Bryk et al., 2015; Knapp, et al, 2014; Wilcox, Angelis & Lawson, 2015).

In the policy implementation research arena the focus has been on top-down and outside-in improvement policies and their respective strategies (e.g., Cohen & Moffitt, 2009; Desimone, 2008; Elmore, 1979; Fullan, 2006). Sometimes these studies examine policies that are "on the drawing board," that is, before they actually are implemented. In addition to dissecting key aspects of the policy design, researchers try to determine the extent to which they are clear, coherent, aligned with others, and research supported (Cobb, Donaldson, & Mayer, 2012).

Other policy studies examine theories-in-use, that is, policies as implemented and enacted (Argyris & Schön, 1996; Cobb, et al., 2012; Honig, 2006), looking expressly at whether these policies are implemented with fidelity, or integrity, and whether they achieve their expressed goals. In other words, they are concerned with whether the policies yield the expected and predicted results in real-world school and district practice. Sometimes these studies address a companion question of whether schools do so efficiently—assessing whether the benefits outweigh the costs.

The three policy innovations at the heart of this book—the CCSS, new APPR systems, and DDI—provide a timely opportunity to join school and district improvement and policy implementation research with improvement science and innovation science, which is just beginning to be done (Coburn, Hill, & Spillane, 2016). This book is not just a collection of findings about odds-beating schools' individual and collective reform and improvement journeys. It also provides timely perspectives regarding policy innovations and how they might disrupt practice in desirable or undesirable ways in different kinds of school systems.

While the three innovations were intended to stimulate desirable and strategic changes to the old model of schooling, like many reform efforts that came before, the intended outcomes have not always been met. Indeed, when innovation is approached too aggressively and without sufficient attention to "good will and engagement of people," the politics of rapid change become a formidable school improvement challenge (Bryk et al, 2015, p. 119).

Learning how to learn to improve in the face of rapid change starts with seeing one's own system and what components of it contribute to its outcomes. In today's turbulent times, learning how to improve also entails accepting an inescapable reality: In contrast to "one and done innovation" that characterized much twentieth-century school reform, in today's world successive innovations are the norm. Part of the challenge of becoming an improvement-oriented, learning organization is that even as the challenges of a current innovation are being addressed, educators must develop readiness for the next disruptive innovation (Christensen, Horn, & Johnson, 2011).

This frame of reference was instrumental in the investigation of the innovations reported on here. The ways that educators in the odds-beating schools and their respective district offices planned for, managed, and learned from policy innovations provided insight into how districts and schools as learning organizations function to reduce the potential for performance declines and increase the potential for improvements to the system during rapid change. At the same time, these district offices' and schools' readiness and capacity for innovations in the here-and-now provide insights into their future developmental trajectories.

The next section takes a step back in history with the intent of establishing a context for the policy innovations investigated and the research findings reported. Two familiar findings introduce the analysis:

- Schools reform over and over again, but they improve very little (Elmore, 2004); and
- The more things have changed the more they have remained the same (Sarason, 1996).

The new science of improvement, together with the movement to refashion district offices and schools as learning organizations, will succeed to the extent that it interrupts the pattern suggested by the above-mentioned, discouraging conclusions.

BREAKING WITH TWENTIETH-CENTURY-REFORM TRADITIONS

The late Peter Drucker (1998) asked, "If we hadn't inherited it, would we do it this way?" He argued that this question opens multiple pathways for innovative designs and also for evidence-based learning, knowledge generation, and continuous improvement. Using the language of the new science of improvement, Drucker's question lays the foundation for efforts by individual schools and interschool networks "to get better at getting better" (Byrk, et al., 2015).

The state's policy innovations—the Common Core standards, new performance-based accountability systems, and data-driven instruction—took aim, in particular, at four inheritances from the twentieth-century model of schooling. Each is described below, with an emphasis on the institutionalized pattern they comprise.

From School Reform to School Improvement

Elmore (2004) provided one story line derived from an impressive body of twentieth-century research and development initiatives. Because reform was a recurrent priority but results did not get better, he emphasized the need to substitute "improvement" for "reform." He also recommended an unrelenting focus on the factors, actors, and strategies that facilitate, constrain, and prevent demonstrable improvements.

Sarason (1996) had earlier described some of these constraints and barriers. Having concluded that "the more things change, the more they remain the same," he identified and described the inherited programmatic and behavioral regularities that served as defining features and maintainers of the status quo of industrial-model schools. These included a reliance on educated guesses rather than reliable, useful data and relevant research to inform reform planning and implementation.

Insufficient Penetration Power: An Unchanging Instructional Core

Life in classrooms tops Sarason's list of fixtures in the industrial-model school. As Tyack and Cuban (1995) quipped, an early twentieth-century teacher could walk into a 1990s classroom and feel right at home, because in both time periods, pedagogy was teacher centered and teacher controlled and classrooms were age graded. At both ends of the century, teachers' isolation in their respective classrooms was conflated with, and justified as, professional autonomy. This arrangement influenced curriculum and instruction, the heart of a schools' core technology: what and how teachers teach and what and how students learn (Lortie, 1975).

Essentially, semi-autonomous teachers could pick their preferred curricula and instructional strategies. This resulted in considerable variability within schools and even within grade levels, with far-ranging consequences. When this pattern prevailed and school and student performance data (and more recently teacher performance data) became more public, parents and students jockeyed to attend the best schools and obtain the best teachers. Variable student outcomes could be attributed in part to the quality of the school overall, "the luck of the draw," or parents' advocacy in students' assignment to a particular teacher.

This situation proved to be a formidable barrier for many school reforms. It helped to explain and justify Tyack and Cuban's (1995) main conclusion that myriad twentieth-century reforms failed to achieve their potential because they remained at the margins of the school (also see Tye, 2000). In other words, most reforms failed to penetrate to the classroom level. Absent desirable changes in schools' core technology of teaching and learning, students' learning experiences and outcomes, as well as teachers' priorities and instructional routines, varied. Policy aspirations for educational equity with demonstrated better student outcomes were not met at scale.

Although Tyack and Cuban (1995) did not discount progress from this reform pattern, they described it as "tinkering toward utopia." Freely translated, reforms at best produced miniature gains and in pockets; many of these pockets were at schools' peripheries instead of classrooms; and the reform process proceeded at glacial speed.

Efficient and Effective School Administration and District Office Management

Focusing on schools' core technology and classrooms tended to privilege teachers as the key systems changers. Granting the importance of this focus, it nevertheless missed significant drivers in the twentieth-century reform agenda. Three of these drivers are especially important: The compelling idea of "a one best system" (Tyack, 1974) was one driver, vestiges of which are evident today. Since the 1960s, at least, considerable investments have been made in standardized and presumably transportable policies, reform models and strategies, and pedagogical practices (Callahan, 1962; Spring, 1976; National Commission on Excellence in Education, 1983).

Another driver was the idea of leadership as management. Preparation programs and performance evaluation systems for superintendents, other district office leaders, and principals were structured accordingly. Granting notable exceptions, status-quo enhancing efficient and effective management trumped leadership for innovation or instruction (Riehl, 2012; Knapp et al, 2014). This management orientation was evident in preparation programs, state certification requirements, and everyday practice.

With efficient management as the priority, even when innovations were implemented, they tended to be approached as "one and done." That is, it was assumed that once a policy or practice had been put in place, the work was done. Such assumptions were predicated on the idea that innovation is an unusual event, ruling out the need for never-ending organizational learning.

A third driver was the development of strong teacher unions, which can be viewed as both a stimulus and a response to managerialism. Beyond salaries and benefits, through their unions teachers sought more voice and choice in their workplaces (Bascia & Osmond, 2012).

High School Graduation as the Goal Line

Twentieth-century industrial-model school systems were designed and operated to produce high school graduates prepared for work and life in an industrial society. Notwithstanding the short-term impacts of economic downturns, for much of the century, assembly line, vocational, and other trade jobs awaited high school graduates and, in some cases, early school leavers. A high school diploma was viewed as a transportable credential that communicated discipline, perhaps more than particular academic competencies and skills.

In this school-driven credentialing system, student classification and sorting systems were the norm. So were explicit and hidden curricular tracking systems that separated college-bound students from their vocational/technical counterparts.

THREE POLICY INNOVATIONS AS GAME-CHANGERS

Since the early 2000s K-12 schools in the United States have experienced a series of federally driven reform agendas. These agendas have emphasized the use of test-based accountability measures to reform schools, as evidenced in the reauthorizations of the Elementary and Secondary Education Act—in 2001, better known as the No Child Left Behind Act, followed in 2015 by the Every Student Succeeds Act.

A centerpiece of the Obama administration's educational policy agenda was an initiative called Race to the Top (RttT). One stated priority of this initiative was the preparation of young people to graduate from high school "college and career ready." This aim encompasses graduates' abilities to demonstrate competence in twenty-first century skills (i.e., critical thinking, communication, collaboration, and creativity) (Partnership for 21st Century Skills, 2008) without need for academic remediation in postsecondary schools.

The initiative sought to engender reform by offering the incentive of substantial competitive grants for states and large school districts that were willing to universally adopt the RttT policy innovations that are the subject of this book (CCSS, APPR, and DDI). Nineteen states, including New York, were awarded such grants.

In brief, in 2009, the CCSS were developed in a collaborative effort between the Council of Chief State School Officers and the National Governors Association (2010). They were purported to have been developed to provide a clear, consistent, and rigorous set of internationally benchmarked standards across grade levels to ensure that all American students are prepared for college and career success.

The CCSS necessitated some specific changes in classroom instruction, defined as "key shifts" (Council of Chief State School Officers & The National Governors Association, 2010). The shifts highlight changes in the breadth and depth of curricular topics as well as increased task complexity. They focus on higher-order thinking skills as well as deep learning of content matter and the use of a range of literacy skills that are transferrable across academic subject areas.

The new Annual Professional Performance Review (APPR) systems required evaluations of teacher and principal practice using a designated set of criteria. Although such evaluations were not new, the criteria under the new APPR included taking into account student achievement based on state assessment data, as well as local test data, in addition to observations of teachers' instruction.

The third leg of the RttT stool rested on data-driven instruction (DDI), which required that districts and schools implement a systematic approach to using student data to improve student learning. This obliged educators to create a cycle of inquiry that included setting student learning objectives (SLOs), determining types of data to collect to assess SLO achievement using those data, and analyzing the data to determine instructional adaptations needed.

From School Improvement to System Innovation

According to those who coined the term "disruptive innovation" (Christensen et al., 2011), the phenomenon always entails learning, because disruptive innovation, when it enjoys sufficient penetration power, ultimately alters an organization's policies, routines, and targeted outcomes (Bryk et al., 2015). Disruptive innovations have the potential to change people's roles, relationships, and responsibilities in tandem with generating new school and district routines (Spillane, 2013).

The public policy priority, then, would be to develop and implement *beneficial* disruptive policy innovations, ones that are fit for purpose in variable contexts as indicated by improved outcomes. In education, one key to the success of such policies might be to ensure that the innovations address the suboptimal features of industrial-model schools described earlier.

Viewed in this way, the policy innovations discussed in this book can be seen as systems interventions, and their effectiveness hinges on several factors, both obvious and hidden. An obvious factor is the extent to which the CCSS, for example, fit the reform/improvement problem needing to be solved: what students learn, how, and when. A hidden one is the readiness and capacity of schools and their district offices to implement or "absorb" one or more disruptive innovations without experiencing performance declines.

If policy innovations are to meet the goal of improving outcomes at scale, they need to meet several specifications:

- End the pattern of "reforming again and again, but improving very little";
- Penetrate the classroom core, ultimately altering and improving what and how teachers teach and what and how students learn;
- Enhance readiness, commitments, and competencies for improvement-oriented practice, particularly leadership for the progressive adoption and implementation of innovations;
- Increase capacities for organizational learning and, in so doing;
- Help schools move toward the ability to get better at getting better.

Returning to the RttT innovations studied in this book, the ultimate target was the instructional core; however, the intended effects of these innovations were meant to be more pervasive than the instructional core. Individually and together, they were structured to alter roles, routines, relationships, and expected performance standards, among other things.

Viewed in this way, these innovations were designed to be system change drivers, with anticipated multiplier and ripple effects, such as the dismissal of teachers and administrators deemed to be ineffective, and even the closure or takeover of poorly performing schools.

Policy Ideals and Implementation Realities

The ability of a school or district to adopt, implement and institutionalize (embed in everyday practice) innovations is known as *absorptive capacity* (e.g., Zahra & George, 2002). This capacity hinges on several interrelated factors, including

- Leadership (broadly defined and distributed);
- Organizational climate;
- Functional working relationships among individuals, teams, and departments;
- Organizational readiness for the specific innovation(s);
- The fit between the innovation(s) and existing structures and operations;
- The characteristics of the innovation implementation strategy;
- Workforce characteristics, especially stability and competence; and
- Prior effectiveness with innovation adoption and implementation.

The logic follows: the better the fit of the innovation to the context, the easier the adoption, implementation, and integration into existing organizational structures and work routines.

While these factors matter in how well an organization can absorb change, so, too, do the qualities of the policy innovations themselves. For example, if a state or federal policy demands innovations requiring considerable shifts from standard practice, or too many innovations in too short a period of time, or innovations that might work at odds with each other (e.g., new high stakes assessments based on new standards and exam-dependent high stakes teacher evaluations), research indicates that some schools may be unable to keep pace, and educators may even attempt to undermine the reform effort (Coburn, Hill, & Spillane, 2016; Cohen & Moffitt, 2009).

Furthermore, since every disruptive innovation depends fundamentally on a tailor-made plan for individual adult (Hall & Hord, 2006) and organizational learning (Knapp, et al., 2014), the absorptive capacity of a school hinges on a resource plan that includes money and time for such learning to occur. When faced with too much change too fast and in the face of limited workforce competencies and insufficient organizational capacity, organizations and individuals may experience innovation overload (Hargreaves & Shirley, 2009).

These circumstances have practical import for school and district leaders, as well as for policymakers and researchers as they decide what to look and listen for as innovations are implemented. For example, districts and schools may have the requisite organizational capacity to absorb innovations such as the CCSS and new performance review requirements because they have invested in new data systems, purchased new instructional technologies, and initiated implementation of innovations that appear to be compatible with new ones.

However, their respective workforces may not yet have the requisite competencies and commitments to successfully implement the innovations or the willingness to do so in the face of what some perceive as a revolving door of reform initiatives that are underfunded and insufficiently supported. Commitment is particularly important when teachers and principals are not merely seen as implementation puppets and when it is crucial that they be ready, willing, and able to change their roles, routines, and relationships.

A UNIQUE AND USEFUL SCHOOL IMPROVEMENT STORY

This book explores what happens in schools that have been able to adapt to disruptive innovations in relatively desirable ways. Overall, it answers major questions such as:

- How and why are educators able to sustain and in some cases improve their overall performance during times of rapid and dramatic innovation?
- What do school and district office leaders prioritize and do to make this happen?
- How do schools and district offices function as learning organizations that support and advance improvements to a school's core technology as they adapt to rapid and dramatic innovation?

The story narrated in these pages extends and expands the dominant tradition of school improvement and effectiveness research in new ways. It provides the "behind the scenes story" of innovation implementation in schools that face the challenges of improving academic performance outcomes among large numbers of ethnically and linguistically diverse children and/or those growing up in poverty. It tells how these schools as learning organizations work relatively effectively because of and also despite rapid innovation implementation challenges.

The remainder of this book shares the findings of a study that identified six patterns of emphasis differentiating odds-beating schools from typically performing ones. As delineated in Chapters 2 through 7, these include:

- A Climate of Trust (Chapter 2)
- Reciprocal Communications (Chapter 3)
- Alignment and Coherence (Chapter 4)
- Readiness for Innovation (Chapter 5)
- Instructional Adaptation (Chapter 6) and
- Whole Child Wellness and Positive Youth Development (Chapter 7)

The descriptions provided in each chapter describe what educators in the odds-beating schools do for themselves and for the student populations they serve. Drawing on the lines of inquiry that provided a common structure to the study, a narrative based on cross-case analyses focuses on interschool patterns regarding proactive and responsive adaptation during a time of rapid, disruptive innovation.

To provide more detailed contextualized accounts, Chapters 2 through 7 also include excerpts from relevant case studies. Chapter 9 provides information about the sampling methodology as well as brief descriptions of each school in the study sample, including demographic data.

Together the chapters tell a story of proactive and adaptive leadership for learning as innovation implementation proceeds. This story includes mechanisms for crafting coherence while maintaining cross-boundary alignments. It describes how educators in odds-beating schools benefit from effective communications systems, trusting and collaborative working relationships, and data-driven learning and improvement systems, extending to how and why teachers have the will and skill to implement innovations and adapt their classroom routines and performances in culturally responsive ways.

These features are summarized in Chapter 8. Framed by the idea of a policy innovation's journey from state education departments to classrooms, this integrative summary has import for policy development and learning, comprehensive district office-school improvement, and future research. Most of all, the findings and conclusions promise to facilitate America's promise to provide equitable, high quality learning and education for the young people who need it most during today's turbulent times.

REFERENCES

Argyris, C., & Schön, D. (1996). *Organizational learning II: Theory, method and practice.* Reading, MA: Addison Wesley.

Bascia, N, & Osmond, P. (2012). *Teacher unions and educational reform: A research review.* Washington, DC: National Education Association. Downloaded from: http://feaweb.org/_data/files/ED_Reform/Teacher_Unions_and_Educational_Reform.pdf

Berger, P., & Luckmann, T. (1967). *The social construction of reality.* New York: Anchor Books.

Brofenbrenner, U. (1993). The ecology of cognitive development: Research models and fugitive findings. In R. H. Wozniak & K. W. Fischer (Eds.), *Development in context: Acting and thinking in specific environments* (pp. 3–44). Hillsdale, NJ: Erlbaum.

Bryk, A., Gomez, L., Grunow, A., & LeMahieu, P. (2015). *Learning to improve: How America's schools can get better at getting better.* Cambridge, MA: Harvard Education Press.

Callahan, R. (1962). *Education and the cult of efficiency.* Chicago: University of Chicago Press.

Christensen, C.M., Horn, M.B., & Johnson, C.W. (2011). *Disrupting class: How disruptive innovation will change the way the world learns.* New York: McGraw Hill.

Cobb, C.D., Donaldson, M. L., & Mayer, A. P. (2012). Creating high leverage policies: A new framework to support policy development. *Berkeley Review of Education*, 4, 265–284. Retrieved from http://escholarship.org/uc/ucbgse_bre.

Coburn, C.E., Hill, H. C., & Spillane, J. P. (2016). Alignment and accountability in policy design and implementation The Common Core State Standards and implementation research. *Educational Researcher*, 45(4), 243–251. doi: 10.3102/0013189x16651080

Cohen, D.K., & Moffitt, S.C. (2009). *The ordeal of inequality: Did federal regulation fit schools?* Cambridge, MA: Harvard University Press.

Council of Chief State School Officers & The National Governors Association (2010). *Common Core State Standards for mathematics and English language arts and literacy in history/social studies, science, and technical subjects.* Washington, DC: National Governors Association. Available at www.corestandards.org.

Coleman, J.S., Campbell, E., Hobson, C., McPartland, J., Mood, F., Weinfeld, F., & York, R.L. (1966). *Equality of educational opportunity.* Washington, DC: U.S. Government Printing Office.

Darling-Hammond, L. (2010). *The flat world and education: How America's commitment to equity will determine our future.* NY: Teachers College Press.

Darling-Hammond, L., & Bransford, J. (Eds.). (2005). *Preparing teachers for a changing world: What teachers should learn and be able to do.* San Francisco, CA: John Wiley & Sons.

Desimone, L.M. (2008). Whole-school change. In M. Shinn & H. Yoshikawa (Eds.), *Toward positive youth development: Transforming schools and community programs* (pp. 150–169). New York: Oxford University Press.

Drucker, P. (1998). Interview with Peter Drucker, C-Span, January.

DuFour, R., & Fullan, M. (2013). *Cultures built to last: Systemic PLCs at work.* Bloomington, IN: Solution Tree Press.

Durand, F.T., Lawson, H.A., Wilcox, K.C., & Schiller, K.S. (2016). The role of proactive and adaptive district leadership in the adoption and implementation of the Common Core State Standards in elementary schools.*Educational Administration Quarterly*, 52(1), 45–74. doi:10.1177/0013161x15615391

Elmore, R. (2004). *School reform from the inside out: Policy, practice, and performance.* Cambridge, MA: Harvard Education Press.

Elmore, R. (1979). Backward mapping: Implementation research and policy decisions. *Political Science Quarterly*, 94(4), 601–616. doi:10.2307/2149628

Fullan, M. (2006). *Turnaround leadership.* San Francisco: Jossey-Bass, Wiley Imprint.

Goldsmith, P.R. (2011). Coleman revisited: School segregation, peers, and frog ponds. *American Educational Research Journal*, 48(3), 508–535. doi: 10.3102/0002831210392019.

Hall, G.E. & Hord, S.M. (2006). *Implementing change: Patterns, principles, and potholes.* Boston: Allyn & Bacon.

Hargreaves, A. & Shirley, D. (2009). The persistence of presentism. *Teachers College Record*, 111(11), 2505–2534.

Hatch, T. (2009). *Managing to change: How schools can survive (and sometimes thrive) in turbulent times.* New York: Teachers College Press.

Honig, M.I. (2006). Complexity and policy implementation: Challenges and opportunities in the field. In M. Honig (Ed.), New directions in educational policy implementation: Confronting complexity (pp. 1–24). Albany, NY: State University of New York Press.

Hopfenberg, W., & Levin, H. (1993). *The accelerated schools resource guide.* San Francisco: Jossey-Bass Publishers.

Knapp, M.S., Copland, M.A., Honig, M.I., Plecki, M.L., & Portin, B.S. (2014). *Practicing and supporting learning-focused leadership in schools and districts.* New York: Routledge.

Lortie, D. (1975). *Schoolteacher: A sociological analysis.* Chicago: University of Chicago Press.

McDonald, J., Klein, E., & Riordan, M. (2009). *Going to scale with new school designs: Reinventing high school.* New York: Teachers College Press.

National Commission on Excellence in Education (1983). *A nation at risk: The imperative for educational reform.* Retrieved November 1, 2002, from http://www.ed.gov/pubs/NatAtRisk/recomm.html

Partnership for 21st Century Skills (2004). *Partnership for 21st Century Skills, Education and competitiveness: A resource and policy guide.* Tucson, AZ: Author.

Porter, M.E.(2008) The five competitive forces that shape strategy. (Special issue on HBS Centennial). *Harvard Business Review* 86(1) (January 2008): 78–93.

Raffo, C. (2014). *Improving educational equity in urban contexts.* New York: Routledge.

Riehl, C. (2012). Edging in: Locating a focus on school-family-community partnerships within the scholarship of educational leadership. In S. Auerbach (Ed.), *School leadership for authentic family and community partnerships: Research perspectives for transforming practice* (pp. 10–28). New York: Routledge.

Rothstein, R. (2004). *Class and schools: Using social, economic and educational reform to close the black-white achievement gap.* Washington, DC: Economic Policy Institute.

Sarason, S. (1996). *The culture of the school and the problem of change revisited.* New York: Teachers College Press.

Slavin, R., Madden, N., Dolan, L., & Wasik, B. (1996). *Every child, every school: Success for all.* Thousand Oaks, CA: Corwin Press.

Spillane, J.P. (2013). The practice of leading and managing teaching in educational organizations. In Organization for Economic and Cooperative Development (Ed.), *Leadership for 21st century learning* (pp. 59–82). Paris: Author.

Spring, J. (1976). *The sorting machine: National educational policy since 1945.* New York: McKay.

Tyack, D. (1974). *The one best system: A history of American urban education.* Cambridge, MA: Harvard University Press.

Tyack, D., & Cuban, L. (1995). *Tinkering toward utopia: A century of public school reform.* Cambridge, MA: Harvard University Press.

Tye, B. (2000). *Hard truths: Uncovering the deep structure of schooling.* New York: Teachers College Press.

Weiner, B.J. (2009). A theory of organizational readiness for change. *Implementation Science*, 4:67. Open Access, Published 19 October 2009. doi:10.1186/1748-5908-4-67.

Wilcox, K.C., & Angelis, J. (2009). *Best practices from high-performing middle schools: How successful schools remove obstacles and create pathways to learning.* New York: Teachers College Press.

Wilcox, K.C., & Angelis, J.I. (2010). *Best practices from high-performing high schools: How successful schools help students stay in school and thrive.* New York: Teachers College Press.

Wilcox, K.C., Angelis, J.I., & Lawson, H. (2015, October). *Developing capacities for evidence-guided continuous improvement: A university/P-12 network project.* Paper presented at the National Center on Scaling Up Effective Schools Annual Conference. Nashville, TN. Vanderbilt Peabody College.

Wilcox, K.C., Lawson, H.A., & Angelis, J.I. (2015). Classroom, school, and district impacts on minority student literacy achievement. *Teachers College Record*, 117(10). Retrieved from http://www.tcrecord.org/content.asp?contentid=18049.

Zahra, S.A., & George, G. (2002). Absorptive capacity: A review, reconceptualization, and extension. *Academy of Management Review*, 27(2), 185–223. doi:10.2307/4134351

Chapter Two

A Climate of Trust

Janet Ives Angelis, Karen Gregory, and Francesca T. Durand

Those who work in organizations that are managed in a rigid, top-down way tend to not trust each other (Lipsky, 1981; McAllister, 1995). In a school system, a lack of trust negatively shapes the interactions not only within schools but also between district- and school-level personnel. It also spills over to affect educators' interactions with students, parents, and the broader community (Thapa et al., 2013).

Trust and transparent communications (see Chapter 3) are two sides of the same coin, and both are necessary for organizational learning and improvement. Trust is also essential for developing individuals' capacities to innovate and improve; high levels of trust, for example, support the collaboration and professional autonomy required for measuring progress toward improvement goals (Lawson et al., 2017) and learning how to get better at getting better (Bryk, Gomez, Grunow, & LeMahieu, 2015).

Rapid, dramatic innovations such as adopting the Common Core State Standards can themselves be emotionally stressful and exacting, so much so that Heifetz (1996) likened the experience of being asked to give up and change pet practices in exchange for new ones as akin to the grief and loss accompanying the death of a loved one. All such events, whether life course or workplace related, are less stressful when people trust each other and are able to give and receive interpersonal supports (Tschannen-Moran, 2014).

Several authors of this book (Lawson et al., 2017) describe trust as needing to flow both horizontally (within a school) and vertically (between school and district). They refer to these relations among educators within a school as *relational* trust, which is contingent on colleagues having confidence in each others' dependability, honesty, competence, and professionalism. Just as essential is *reciprocal* trust, the relations between school-level educators and district office personnel. Relational trust is a key boundary-crossing lubricant discussed in more detail in Chapter 8.

Many studies have linked relational trust with student performance. A key work is Bryk and Schneider's (2002) decade-long study of the effort to reform Chicago's public elementary schools. Using both qualitative and quantitative measures, their analyses showed a clear gap in terms of improved student performance in both reading and mathematics between schools with high levels of relational trust and those that lacked such trust. Other studies (e.g., Kraft, Marinell, & Yee, 2016; Meier, 1995; Cook, Murphy, & Hunt, 2000; Wilcox & Angelis, 2011) lend further evidence of the trust–performance connection across middle and high schools.

Reciprocal trust complements relational trust and is essential to district efforts to support improved outcomes at the school level (Lawson et al., 2017). When leaders of organizations in which trust is lacking attempt to standardize performance by resorting to top-down, compliance-oriented structures that individuals are expected to follow, they further erode trust (McAllister, 1995). This approach is unlikely to lead to successful implementation of new practices or the desired outcomes (Lawson et al., 2017).

Both relational and reciprocal trust were demonstrated in the odds-beating schools in this study in some distinct ways in comparison to the typically performing schools. This was true both for relations within and between the school and district and those between the school/district and its community, including students' families. Most significantly, trusting relations differed in both quality and prevalence between the groups of schools.

This chapter turns its attention to these differences, first to relations within schools and districts and then to relations with students, families, and the broader community. It closes with two cases in point, an elementary school that provides a strong example of trusting relations within the school and district and a middle school that demonstrates trusting relations with the community.

TRUSTING RELATIONS WITHIN THE
SCHOOL AND DISTRICT

Relations within any organization are interdependent, what Weick (1979) termed a "double interact." What one party does (or does not do) influences how the other reacts. Tied up in these interactions are aspects of and perceptions of respect, personal regard, competence, and personal integrity (Bryk & Schneider, 2002; Robinson, 2010). All trust, then, must be two-way: it defines relations between individuals; it is socially constructed and serves to "[bind] individuals together to advance the education and welfare of students" (Bryk & Schneider, 2003, p. 44).

Another way to put it is that trust is the "soft tissue" (Wilcox, Lawson, & Angelis, 2015, p. 28) of an organization, involving both reason and emotions (McAllister, 1995; Tschannen-Moran & Hoy, 2000). To trust is to be vulnerable, and to be trusted means to be transparent about motives, successes, and challenges (Wilcox & Angelis, 2011; Tschannen-Moran & Gareis, 2015a & b).

Providing the psychological safety for staff to innovate and to receive and make use of meaningful feedback even in the face of failures contributes to building and sustaining both relational and reciprocal trust. So, too, does expressing confidence in a staff's competence to try new approaches (Bryk, Sebring, Allensworth, Luppescu, & Easton, 2009; Kutsyuruba & Walker, 2014; Lawson et al., 2017).

One challenge for school leaders is to establish an environment with enough trust to provide safety for teachers and support staff to be willing to take the risks necessary to innovate. In the study being reported on here, not only were teachers expected to change their performance—by using new data systems to inform instruction and to teach to the Common Core standards—but also their performance evaluations were to be based, in part, on how their students performed on Common Core assessments. This was a high-risk, high-stress situation.

Educators in the odds-beating schools displayed higher levels of trust than their counterparts in the typical performers, including the resulting confidence to make professional judgments about how best to innovate to meet new requirements. This trust was evident in the way teachers and other support staff expressed respect for one another, the honesty they brought to their work and their collaborations, and in the sense of security and safety they described feeling. For example, they expressed a level of comfort with productive failure—that learning from failure was acceptable and even expected in order to learn to get better at getting better.

In the schools with higher levels of reciprocal and relational trust, the process of innovation implementation was smoother and the results in terms of student performance on Common Core assessments stronger. The following sections discuss, first, some of the deliberate steps that leaders had taken to create a climate of trust. This is followed by a discussion showing how such trust resulted in feelings of professionalism among teachers, who were willing to undertake the changes required to implement the new policies.

Building a Climate Conducive to Trust

Leaders who described their efforts to establish conditions conducive to trust told about prioritizing trusting environments, distributing leadership, encouraging multidirectional communications and contacts, listening, and generally creating a safe environment to share failures, successes, and ideas for improvement. As the principal of Starling Springs ES put it, "[I] can't lead anything unless there's a high level of trust between the staff and me, because if that's not there . . . , really kind of nothing else matters. That's sort of like the bedrock foundation."

Similarly, the principal of Roaring Gap MS explained that trust and safety are essential to being able to give teachers feedback that they can hear and respond to with the desire and intent to improve. "Nobody hears it if it's not safe," she said.

Teachers in the odds-beating schools told about some of the specific ways in which principals supported their efforts and provided the building blocks for establishing and maintaining trust. These included offering a clear vision of desired performance, being knowledgeable and fair, and expressing confidence in teachers' competencies. A teacher at Eagle Bluff ES described her principal in this way:

> She is very supportive and that makes me feel like I can go in and ask [for] this and if I can't do it, fine, but I'm not afraid to do that because she's just so supportive. And . . . she'll tell you that she is going to be [supportive] as long as we do our part.

Teachers at Goliad ES made similar comments about their principal, saying, "She trusts our expertise," and "She treats everyone respectfully; she's fair."

In some typically performing schools, the principal was described as supportive, but not in a consistent way. At Sun Hollow ES, for example, one teacher described the principal as supportive in some ways, especially when it came to children's needs, but not in others, particularly with regard to relating to families. She explained, "If there's an issue with an actual student, I find I have more support, but if it's an issue with a parent, sometimes it could be better."

This example highlights the connection between trust and working together to tackle the very challenging work of adopting new practices. At the district level, central office staff of the odds-beating schools expressed the belief that the success of the district is reliant upon partnerships. For example, the assistant superintendent of curriculum and instruction at Goliad ES said,

> I think first and foremost . . . that we must partner with schools. My leadership is partnering. I must partner with schools. I must partner with individual principals. I must partner with my other colleagues. I must partner with the state. I must partner with my consultants. I see this work as the work of a partnership.

Trust and Professional Discretion

A common refrain of district leaders of odds-beating schools was that teachers are the classroom experts and that they should be trusted to implement a standards-aligned curriculum effectively. Perhaps, more important, they backed up this idea in a variety of ways, such as offering useful professional development, restructuring time and resources for teachers to discuss and plan standards-aligned lessons, and providing consistent messages about expectations and professional evaluations.

In the middle schools in which instructional coaches support teachers to adopt new instructional strategies in line with new standards, teachers credited coaches with building trust as they engaged in embedded professional development. For example, a Roaring Gap MS instructional coach reported that her honest constructive feedback to teachers was both reliant on trust and also a benefit:

> Have I had to have some frank conversations? Absolutely. But I feel like I can do that now because I have developed the relationship to say, "Time out; let's just talk about this. I know it feels uncomfortable. Personally, my personal growth happens when I'm uncomfortable."

And at Laribee MS, an instructional coach asserted a similar explicit intent to respectfully and personally relate to teachers in her building.

> I always think you try and treat others the way you would want to be treated. . . . I try to have personal connections with people. I'll very often go out of my way to meet with people in person or to touch base with them in classrooms to catch them, as opposed to sending an e-mail or sending a memo. I almost never send memos."

In contrast, typically performing schools were characterized by more inconsistent profiles in the relational trust evident between adults. Some educators described operating with little connection to others, and a few expressed outright distrust of people with whom they worked. Although in the typically performing schools, most teachers reported trusting their school leaders and each other, this trust did not always relate to working collaboratively. Instead, teachers described acting largely independently of colleagues.

The biggest distinction between odds-beating and typically performing schools with regard to trust came from the level of reciprocal trust evident between district leaders and school-level staff. In typically performing schools, although district leaders often stated that they trusted the expertise of teachers and principals, teachers did not reciprocate this sense of trust in district leaders.

For example, at typically performing Paige City ES, teachers reported working together and trusting their principal to support them, but they expressed apprehension and, in some cases, even fear regarding district staff's view of their performance reviews. Teachers' anxiety was acknowledged by a district administrator, who reported a notable increase in counseling services for "teachers who experience what they perceive as a lot of stress based on what they're being asked to do and how they're being evaluated and not knowing what that means for them in their job."

This lack of clarity relates in part to the qualities and modes of communication between district offices and schools, as discussed in more detail in Chapter 3. It also relates to what teachers felt was inadequate and/or inappropriate professional development. This sense of feeling unprepared was voiced as a significant source of stress for teachers, which was most notable in typically performing schools. For example, a teacher from Sun Hollow ES explained,

> There's such a pressure to understand what they're wanting us to teach, and then we have to go to what they've given us to teach [the state's Common Core curriculum modules] and how, and figure it out and create a workbook and make sure it's hitting all of our kids—and that's like where it's been a struggle. You're paddling and you keep sinking, and you [think], "OK, let's get to the surface." And you sink again because you get ahead and then . . . "We're in a new module," and we've got to go through it all again.

In sum, three characteristics of professional support that nurtured trust during the implementation of the Common Core standards and related innovations included: (1) clear communications about expectations for performance from district offices to the school; (2) sufficient professional development in anticipation of the implementation of the innovations (i.e., crafting readiness for innovation); and (3) personalized, respectful, and constructive feedback from instructional coaches.

Individually and together these features affected teachers' perceptions of how safe—and trusted—they felt to make professional judgments about curriculum and instruction during implementation of the Common Core standards, new professional performance review systems, and data-driven instruction.

DEVELOPING TRUST WITH PARENTS AND COMMUNITY

Studies consistently demonstrate that consistent, open, and two-way communication builds trust not only within schools and districts but also with parents and the broader community (e.g., Bryk et al., 2009; Notman & Henry, 2011; Robinson, 2010; Wilcox & Angelis, 2011). In turn, this trust can lead to collaboration with families and community groups, which has been shown to support school engagement, classroom engagement, academic learning, and academic performance (e.g., Hill & Tyson, 2009; Lawson & Lawson, 2013; O'Sullivan, Yung-Chi, and Fish, 2014; Sheldon & Epstein, 2005).

In their study at the middle level, for example, Hill and Tyson (2009) found a positive relation between parental involvement and student achievement. This involvement shifted from helping their children with their homework and assisting in the elementary classroom to attending school activities and building communication with teachers.

While educators across the nation agree about the benefit of family engagement for academic success, researchers find that many educators lack preparation to work with students' families (Epstein & Sanders, 2006; Mapp & Kuttner, 2013). They may employ traditional strategies such as bake sales, school nights, and parent–teacher conferences to engage parents, but parent participation in those events is low, especially in schools that serve low-income families (Bower & Griffin, 2011; Mapp & Kuttner, 2013; Schutz, 2006).

Weiss and colleagues (2010) attribute the phenomena of low parent engagement to the lack of integration and alignment between typical engagement activities and school improvement efforts. The absence of systematic and coordinated plans leads to random efforts to engage parents—episodic meetings and events that have limited influence on learning outcomes.

All schools in this study confronted the challenges of educating students growing up in poverty, and both odds-beating and typically performing schools displayed similarities in their attempts to form partnerships to help them address those challenges. What differed was that the efforts in the odds-beating schools were more systematic and involved two-way communication channels (see Chapter 3). Other differences were found in the levels of understanding and respect expressed by educators for parents and families, as well as the extent of leadership support for such engagement.

Respect for Family and Community

As discussed in Chapters 6 and 7, educators in the odds-beating schools worked to meet the learning and social-emotional needs of individual students. So, too they sought to take into account diverse family backgrounds and experiences. In Starling Springs ES, for example, leaders spoke of being especially mindful of parents who themselves may not have had positive experiences with schooling:

> If I'm going outside and there's a family here who . . . do lots of great things for the school and they're kind of more in that mainstream culture and a family here where the kid might be struggling a little and parents might not have had a great experience in school, I'm probably going to the family that's at risk of

feeling or being marginalized first just in terms of chatting with them or connecting with them.

In contrast, educators at typically performing schools tended to describe their students' and their families' poverty, transience, or disengagement as serious impediments to teaching and learning. For example, a district administrator for Paige City ES discussed how the demographics of their community had become a "piece of blame" in the district's struggle to raise student achievement:

> [The school] is a challenging place. It has a changing demographic from the past 20 years. The transient mobility rate inside it is high. What I've found is the district commonly talked about the changing demographics all the time when I was being hired, when I was being interviewed, and then in my entrance plan. What they didn't tell me is that they hadn't done anything about it. . . . I was shocked that no one had done much about it to the point of blaming [this change] anytime it came to accountability or results. . . . That was seven years ago.

In contrast, when educators at odds-beating schools talked about their students' needs, deficit or blaming language was rarely used. While understanding the many challenges that certain students face, the words of an administrator at Starling Springs ES demonstrate the emphasis that educators in odds-beating schools place on seeing the child beyond the test score:

> They [students] are not just a test score or a grade level; they're a whole person that has emotions, has social developmental challenges along with their academics. . . . So some of the things we talked about were how do we engage children that are having a difficult life? I mean there's really no other way to say it. Maybe they're academically fine but they may be emotionally numb because of what's going on in their house. So if a kid has an interest in horseback riding and that's kind of the shining light in their life, who would you contact in this county that could help you connect with that kid?

District administrators, and in some cases principals, play a key role in hiring teachers and developing their skills to match the needs of their school populations. Among the odds-beating schools, district and school administrators spoke about specific attributes they look for in teachers. At Yellow Valley ES, for example, the principal stated that he looks for someone who understands the challenges of poverty but can see beyond poverty and hold high standards.

This sentiment was echoed by the assistant principal, who said that they look for an understanding of poverty and family differences from teachers to lunch monitors. A district leader stated that the school has "a culture . . . that identifies with children of poverty. They have built upon [it], used their professional development. . . . They're truly a group that believes those kids can learn."

Collaborative and Supportive Leadership for Family Engagement

Leadership has a significant impact on both how sustainable and integrated parent/family engagement is (Leithwood, Patten, & Jantzi, 2010; Weiss et al., 2010). Leaders' roles are not necessarily to meet directly with parents, but rather to orchestrate efforts that can make it possible (Ishimaru, 2013) and place parents on the school improvement agenda (Mapp & Kuttner, 2013).

Leaders of odds-beating schools demonstrated more focused support of family engagement efforts than those of typically performing schools. Additionally, leaders in odds-beating schools and districts described alternative ways of meeting student needs and goals, including working with community partners, applying for grants, restructuring roles of staff, and closely reviewing budgets and needs.

At odds-beating Hutch Hill MS, teachers suggested that family engagement in the school resulted from a collective effort. As one said, "Our school is very good about recognizing, engaging, and delivering things that those families need. I mean I'm always amazed at all the different efforts that collectively this building does for students and families of students."

Similar indications of collaborative efforts to engage parents were also found in odds-beating Sage City MS, where published newsletters distributed to parents are written in both English and Spanish. District leaders work with the school to ensure that families are receiving consistent messages from both the school and the district office. A district leader explained,

> Anything written to parents goes home in English and Spanish. . . . Sometimes they need help with wording or how to ensure that it's in line with the district philosophy, or sometimes we'll say to the building, "I know you're having a newsletter coming out soon, I need you to include this." That way everyone sees what's happening at the district level.

This culturally relevant approach to family engagement enhances not only trust, but also the social and emotional health of students, as discussed in Chapter 7.

Especially at the middle level, teachers in odds-beating schools are encouraged to have web pages that families can access and use. In Julesberg, for example, the district provides support for teachers to do so, including offering stipends to create videos.

Leaders of odds-beating schools also take the initiative to reach out to the broader community. At Hutch Hill MS, the district was working on plans to develop school-linked and school-based services via a partnership with a local mental health agency. In Julesberg MS, a district administrator, reported:

> I go to all of the community association meetings. I go to fire department board meetings and all the commission meetings—just meet with them. . . . They are organizations here that have a disproportionate influence on what happens in the school, because either they literally donate something, or work with us, or they're just organizations that are so well respected that people like to see the same affection between organizations they respect as they do between individuals they respect.

Educators in some of the typically performing schools also described efforts to engage parents and families, but these efforts were often sporadic, dependent on individual initiative, and/or not underwritten or supported by building or district leadership. For example, in Silver City MS, parents were invited to attend sessions on academic, health, and wellness themes, taught by teachers and school counselors. But this program was episodic rather than ongoing.

Added to that, the effort to reach out to parents was dependent on individual initiative, as indicated by the following statement from a Silver City ESL teacher:

> I personally see the parents twice in a quarter and I call . . . once a week. That is the nature of my job. I just tend to talk a lot with parents. It's just easier for me, and now with [a tablet computer] . . . we do a lot of [video call] and texting. So it's made it very convenient and it happens. It just happens.

But "it just happens" because of this teacher's individual initiative. Her strategy for reaching out to parents was neither organized nor mandated by school leaders. Having leadership support for this kind of family engagement is another factor that distinguishes odds-beating from typically performing schools.

Not only were narratives indicating leadership support for collaborative and collective efforts for parent engagement relatively absent in the typically performing schools, but also their leaders did not necessarily see that as a negative. In Tarelton MS, for example, the superintendent gave one reason for lack of involvement:

> In a rural school that has a high poverty rate—and most of the parents we have are former students here . . . but one of the things about public education is that most educators get under the gun sometimes because people have had an experience with [it]. . . . So you know when you go to a doctor you don't question what your doctor says and you don't question what your lawyer says because you never went to law school and you didn't go to med school, but you went to

K-12 school, so you have an opinion about what happens in education, and not all the experiences people had were good.

Now teachers I hope had a positive experience in their educational upbringing because otherwise they wouldn't be teachers. But you have to understand that they may be dealing with parents that had a negative experience. . . . And that experience comes to them; they are reminded of that experience every time they walk through our door.

And a building leader at typically performing Locust Glen MS also noted that limited parent involvement in school and classroom is to be expected:

With regards to parents actually coming in and helping in classrooms, we see that decline drastically at middle school. I think part of the reason why is frankly [students] don't want their parents in here . . . they really want to be separate sometimes and they're real happy that they leave the elementary and come to the middle school. And it's interesting, parents kind of have a tendency, and I don't know if it's good or bad, but they will back off there a little bit.

Hill and Tyson (2009) and O'Sullivan and colleagues (2014) argue that while the form of parent involvement at the middle level is different from that in elementary school, school–family relations at this level are no less important for academic success. Yet, at typically performing Tarelton and Locust Glen, parent engagement was not a priority. In addition, the dominant narratives were primarily about difficulties in engaging parents instead of supporting them.

Overall, distinctions between the odds-beating and typically performing schools in terms of trusting relations with families and the broader community were related to understanding of, empathy with, and respect for students' families, especially immigrants and those living in poverty; and the extent to which leaders supported and coordinated outreach and communications. Chapter 3 provides additional details about reciprocal communications, the flip side of the trust–communications coin.

A CASE IN POINT—SPRING CREEK ELEMENTARY SCHOOL

We have teachers that work together very well, who support each other and help each other out whenever we need to. Everybody works together here.

—teacher

District leaders at Spring Creek Elementary emphasized frequent, clear communication, shared responsibility, and giving teachers and other staff considerable discretion in how they proceed with their work. The superintendent was said to set the tone, and her self-reported leadership style and strategies fit with what others reported.

She portrayed herself as having high expectations for everyone in the district and reported how pleased she is when someone repeats one of her ideas to her as their own. That, she said, indicated ownership of the idea. Individual and focus group interviews with staff indicated that this leadership strategy and philosophy were understood and welcomed. She emphasized that she prioritized having the highest possible standards and expectations for all students and that these expectations need to be the same for students who receive free or reduced-price lunch—about half the school's student population.

Anticipating state-mandated changes such as annual professional performance reviews based on Common Core assessments, she said that she had worked with the board and leadership team to lay the groundwork so that the staff would be ready. For example, the district started the new teacher evaluation process the year before it was required. She reported meeting regularly with teachers and parents, seeking evaluative feedback, then working with her leadership team to use this feedback and develop consensus.

The district curriculum coordinator, a teacher on special assignment, corroborated the superintendent's statement that when administrators decided to adopt some of the state modules, they made it known to teachers that they were trusted to make instructional decisions. Teacher comments further substantiated claims that all staff members, especially teachers, regularly are asked by the superintendent, principal, and other administrators what they need to successfully implement the Common Core standards. Many teachers mentioned that administrators conveyed the message that teachers are trusted to do what is best for their students.

Leadership at the school falls mostly on the principal, who stated that he and the superintendent work closely together and have worked to align their goals and improvement strategies. At the same time, the principal shares leadership responsibilities with staff members, letting them know that he respects their professional judgment and encouraging them to jointly steward Spring Creek Elementary School (Case in Point from Wilcox et al., 2014).

A CASE IN POINT—SAGE CITY MIDDLE SCHOOL

It is a middle school so . . . communicating with parents—not just, "Your son was late today to school; this is his seventh lateness," but also . . . "I was in math class today and I saw your son doing a ninth-grade math problem and I just wanted to say, 'Hats off, and he is doing a really great job.'" . . . just some sort of positive phone calls home as well—I think that that's important in building relationships with parents and making myself available with any questions or concerns that anybody in the community has.

—assistant principal

District and school leaders, teachers, and staff at Sage City value and prioritize family and community engagement. At the district level, the superintendent holds monthly informal meetings with parents and community members in both English and Spanish. Administrators also described making it a point to attend all school events and taking parents' opinions into account when making district-wide decisions.

The district also supports the school in developing strong and positive relations with families. Interview and focus group discussions with a variety of personnel revealed that educators share common values and beliefs about family engagement. As at any school, difficulty in encouraging some parents to be more involved was indeed a part of the narrative; however, Sage City educators maintain constant efforts to build positive relations and in-person, two-way communication because they believe families have an influential role in education.

All families—regardless of their cultural and academic backgrounds—are invited to various school activities, including concerts, drama performances, and art shows. Beyond those events, the school attempts to keep parents informed through community meetings, quarterly assessment reports, awards assemblies, open houses, and a general open-door policy.

School leaders, teachers, and staff consistently communicated about issues related to the new curriculum and testing so that educators and parents had shared visions and common understanding about the implementation of the new curriculum. The principal maintained that because parents are informed, they appreciate the school's efforts, adding,

> Parents understand the complexities of, and they understand the importance of Common Core. . . . I totally believe in setting the standards high and in the Common Core work. I believe that we have to make sure that kids are college- and career-ready by the time they graduate high school, and I think that parents believe that as well.

Parents are not only expected to support their children's learning at home and attend events and meetings held by the school, but to also inform school-level decisions about their children's learning and academic progress. Parents are asked to submit an input letter before or as the school year begins, so that the school has a sense of any social or emotional needs of the child and anything (or any services) that the school might need to provide. Hence, parents have the opportunity to influence the learning process.

Efforts to engage families and communities, an assistant superintendent said, are grounded on needs. To address poverty-related barriers to learning, the school has established partnerships with various organizations and mental health service providers. Parents were reported to trust educators and to feel secure about consulting with school support staff about their children's development. A member of the support staff in a focus group discussion gave an example:

> Parents will often say they're at wits end dealing with a preteen. Where do they begin? So we help them in . . . the parenting skill set of establishing rules and routines and schedules at home that will help the parent to engage the child and get them to get the homework done.

The assistant principal encourages teachers to maintain communication with parents at any time and to inform parents not only about problems their children have at school, but also about positive behaviors. The frequent information sessions with parents about changes to testing and curriculum helped parents to share their concerns, and they allowed teachers to respond to them. One school leader explained that this process demonstrated the school culture: "I think that again it speaks to the culture here. We're just good about responding to our public. You know, without their support we have nothing." (Case in Point from Wilcox et al., 2015).

SUMMARY

Overall, a clear distinction between odds-beating and typically performing schools and their districts was evident with regard to school and district climates of trust. Educators in the odds-beaters already had established and continually cultivated the conditions conducive to positive relations and interactions. They showed evidence of reciprocal trust between the schools and their districts as well as relational trust within each. And they clearly believed that trusting in one another, giving each other the freedom and safety to make judgments about practice, and school leadership's role in promoting a climate of trust were critical to the functioning of their school.

Conversely, educators in typically performing schools showed evidence of inconsistent trust between educators. Some expressed a trust in others' judgment and expertise, but did not demonstrate it in action; others explicitly articulated that they did not believe that leaders were supportive of their work. Additionally, leaders in typically performing schools did not provide clear guidelines to faculty about using their professional judgment as they tried to innovate to meet new policy requirements. Inconsistencies in messaging about professional discretion were particularly damaging to reciprocal trust.

As for extending a climate of trust from within school and district outward to parents and the broader community, this study found a difference between the odds-beaters and the typical performers; this was especially true for the schools serving low-income families and minority groups. The efforts of educators in the odds-beaters to improve parent engagement was supported by leadership and grounded in respect for parents and families as well as the premise that they needed support from the parents. They also recognized the need to help parents so that they could effectively support their children.

Instead of one-way communication, educators in odds-beating schools systematically attempted to build and maintain positive relationships and two-way, constructive communications with parents, led and supported by leadership at both district and school levels. Chapter 3 describes in greater detail how school and district leaders fostered reciprocal communications.

REFERENCES

Bryk, A.S., Sebring, P.B., Allensworth, E., Luppescu, S., & Easton, J.Q. (2009). *Organizing schools for improvement: Lessons from Chicago.* Chicago: Chicago University Press.

Bryk, A.S., & Schneider, B.L. (2002). *Trust in schools: A core resource for improvement.* New York: Russell Sage.

—— (2003). Trust in schools: A core resource for school reform. *Educational Leadership* 60(6), 41–44.

Bryk, A., Gomez, L., Grunow, A., & LeMahieu, P. (2015). *Learning to improve: How America's schools can get better at getting better.* Cambridge, MA: Harvard Education Press.

Cook, T.D., Murphy, R.F., & Hunt, H.D. (2000). Comer's School Development Program in Chicago: A theory-based evaluation. *American Educational Research Journal*, 37(2), 535–97.

Epstein, J.L., & Sanders, M.G. (2006). Prospects for change: Preparing educators for school, family, and community partnerships. *Peabody Journal of Education*, 81(2), 81–120. doi:10.1207/s15327930pje8102_5

Fullan, M. (2006). *Turnaround leadership.* San Francisco: Jossey-Bass, Wiley Imprint.

Heifetz, R. (1994). *Leadership without easy answers.* Cambridge, MA: Belknap Press.

Henderson, A.T., Mapp, K, Johnson, V., & Davies, D. (2007). *Beyond the bake sale: The essential guide to family-school partnerships.* New York: The New Press.

Hill, N.E. & Tyson, D.F. (2009). Parental involvement in middle school: A meta-analytic assessment of the strategies that promote achievement. *Developmental Psychology*, 45(3), 740–763. doi:10.1037/a0015362

Ishimaru, A. (2013). From heroes to organizers: Principals and education organizing in urban school reform. *Educational Administration Quarterly*, 49(1), 3–51. doi:10.1177/0013161x12448250

Kraft, M.A., Marinell, W.H., & Yee, D. (2016). Schools as organizations: Examining school climate, teacher turnover, and student achievement in NYC. New York: Research Alliance for New York City Schools. (http://steinhardt.nyu.edu/scmsAdmin/media/users/sg158/PDFs/schools_as_organizations/SchoolsAsOrganizations_PolicyBrief.pdf)

Kutsyuruba, B., & Walker, K. (2014). The life cycle of trust in educational leadership: An ecological perspective. *International Journal of Educational Leadership: Theory and Practice*. doi: 10. 1080/13603124. 2014. 915061

Lawson, H.A., Durand, F.T, Wilcox, K.C., Gregory, K., Schiller, K. S., & Zuckerman, S (2017). The role of district and school leaders' trust and communications in the simultaneous implementation of policy innovations. *Journal of School Leadership*, 27(1).

Lawson, M. & Lawson, H.A. (2013). New conceptual frameworks for student engagement research, policy, and practice. *Review of Educational Research*, 83(3), 432–479. doi:10.3102/0034654313480891

Leithwood, K., Patten, S., & Jantzi, D. (2010). Testing a conception of how school leadership influences student learning. *Educational Administration Quarterly*, 46(5), 671–706. doi: 10. 1177/0013161X10377347

Lipsky, M. (1980). Street-level bureaucracy: Dilemmas of the individual in public services. New York: Russell Sage Foundation.

Mapp, K., & Kuttner, P. (2013). Partners in education: A dual capacity-building framework for family-school partnerships. SEDL in collaboration with the U. S. Department of Education. Retrieved from http://www2.ed.gov/documents/family-community/partners-education.pdf.

McAllister, D. (1995). Affect- and cognition-based trust as foundations for interpersonal cooperation in organizations. *Academy of Management Journal*, 38(1), 24–59. doi:10.2307/256727

Meier, D. (1995). *The power of their ideas: Lessons for America from a small school in Harlem.* Boston: Beacon Press.

Notman, R., & Henry, D.A., (2011). Building and sustaining successful school leadership in New Zealand. *Leadership and Policy in Schools*, 10(4), 375–394. doi: 10.1080/15700763.2011.610555

O'Sullivan, R. H., Yung-Chi, C., & Fish, M.C. (2014). Parental mathematics homework involvement of low-income families with middle school students. *School Community Journal*, 24(2), 165–187.

Robinson, V.M.J. (2010). From instructional leadership to leadership capabilities: Empirical findings and methodological challenges. *Leadership and Policy in Schools* 9(1), 1–26. doi: 10. 1080/15700760903026748

Schutz, A. (2006). Home is a prison in the global city: The tragic failure of school-based community engagement strategies. *Review of Educational Research*, 76(4), 691–743. doi:10.3102/00346543076004691

Senge, P., Cambron-McCabe, N., Lucas, T., Smith, B., Dutton, J., & Kleiner, A. (2012). *Schools that learn*. 2nd Edition. New York: Crown Business.

Thapa, A. Cohen, J., Guffey, S., & Higgins-D'Alessandro, A. (2013). A review of the school climate research. *Review of Educational Research*, on-line first. April 19, 2013. doi:10.3102/0034654313483907

Tschannen-Moran, M. (2014). *Trust matters: Leadership for successful schools*. San Francisco: Jossey-Bass.

Tschannen-Moran, M. & Gareis, C.R. (2015a). Faculty trust in the principal: An essential ingredient in high performing schools. *Journal of Educational Administration*, 53(1), 66–92. doi:10.1108/jea-02-2014-0024

Tschannen-Moran, M. & Gareis, C.R. (2015b). Principals, trust, and cultivating vibrant schools. Societies, 5, 256–276. doi:10.3390/soc5020256

Tschannen-Moran, M., & Hoy, W. (2000). A multidisciplinary analysis of the nature, meaning, and measurement of trust. *Review of Educational Research*, 70(4), 547–593. doi:10.3102/00346543070004547

Weick, K.E. (1979). *The social psychology of organizing (2nd ed.)*. Reading, MA: Addison-Wesley.

Weiss, H.B., Lopez, M.E., & Rosenberg, H. (2010). *Beyond random acts: Family, school, and community engagement as an integral part of education reform*. Cambridge, MA: Harvard Family Research Project.

Wilcox, K.C., & Angelis, J.I. (2011). *Best practices from high-performing high schools: How successful schools help students stay in school and thrive*. New York: Teachers College Press.

Wilcox, K.C., Durand, F.T., Gregory, K., Schiller, K.S., Lawson, H., Zuckerman, S., Felicia, N., & Angelis, J.I. (2015*). Odds-beating middle schools cross-case report*. Prepared for the New York State Education Department as part of the School Improvement Study. Albany, NY: State University of New York.

Wilcox, K.C., Durand, F.T., Schiller, K.S., Gregory, K. Zuckerman, S., Felicia, N., Angelis, J.I., & Lawson, H. (2014*). Odds-beating elementary school cross-case report*. Prepared for the New York State Education Department as part of the School Improvement Study. Albany, NY: State University of New York.

Wilcox, K.C., Lawson, H.A., & Angelis, J.I. (2015). Classroom, school and district impacts on minority student literacy achievement. *Teachers College Record*, 117(10). Retrieved from http://www.tcrecord.org/content.asp?contentid=18049

Chapter Three

Reciprocal Communications

Francesca T. Durand

When the Common Core State Standards (CCSS), new annual professional performance review (APPR) systems, and data-driven instruction (DDI) were simultaneously rolled out, district and school leaders faced considerable challenges with regard to how to use communications to help effect the required changes. These communications would not only need to provide staff with clear and accurate information about the content of the innovations themselves, but also secure everyone's support for implementing them. Communications would need to be responsive to educators' needs to make sense of the innovations as the process of implementation proceeded.

Articulating manageable timelines for, specific requirements of, and expectations for fidelity of implementation also presented communications challenges. State education department officials largely relied on turnkey models to communicate about the innovations themselves, leading to some misinformation as the information journeyed from state policy drawing boards to schools. Further, policy revisions after initial announcements required that school and district leaders continuously interpret these changes and how to best inform staff without creating confusion and disintegrating hard-won trust in their leadership, as discussed in Chapter 2.

Additionally, leaders faced a history of innovation fatigue and its predictable and associated side effect of resistance, as teachers faced yet another reform effort, this one with particularly high-stakes consequences (Fullan, 2006), particularly the use of student scores on Common Core assessments as part of their professional evaluations. Leaders, then, had to choose whether to use a top-down, one-way approach that viewed the innovations as policy transfers to be implemented with fidelity or an approach that invited multiway communications and problem solving (Datnow, 2006; Fullan, 2006; Honig, 2004).

This chapter focuses on two primary questions related to the role of communications in supporting the implementation of the innovations in odds-beating and typically performing schools: 1) How were communications used in odds-beating schools and their districts to support implementation of innovations? and 2) How did communications differ in the typically performing schools and districts? The next section offers a brief review of prior related research about how educators, particularly educational leaders, create effective communication systems and use various forms of communication to support organizational innovation and learning.

PERFORMANCE ADAPTATION AND COMMUNICATION

Reciprocal (i.e., two-way) communication has been identified as a critical component of leadership, especially during times of rapid change (Durand, Lawson, Wilcox, & Schiller, 2016; Elmore, 2004; Honig, 2014; Honig & Copland, 2014; Knapp, Honig, Plecki, Portin, & Copland, 2014, Lawson, et al., 2017). However, as has been found in prior research, in organizations undergoing change, leaders face structural, interpersonal, and alignment challenges (Honig, 2004; Leithwood & Sun, 2012), and sometimes internal resistance (Fullan, 2006).

Scholars have pointed to qualities of learning organizations that implicate the importance of communications in meeting these challenges. These include studies that focus on the role of communications in interdependent relationships (Elmore, 2004), defined autonomy among expert professional educators (also see Chapter 5) (Marzano & Waters, 2009), and cultures of learning organizations (Knapp et al., 2014). Some of the qualities of communications that are of particular import are the degree of clarity, channels used, the multiway flow, and framing challenges as an opportunity for improvement (Marzano, 2003).

Educators who prioritize communications and trust building (see Chapter 2) facilitate not just the day-to-day management of their district or school, but also the implementation of innovative reform policies (Lawson et al., 2017). They are able to provide leadership for learning.

USING COMMUNICATIONS TO SUPPORT
INNOVATION IN ODDS-BEATING SCHOOLS

In the odds-beating schools, communications were used to ease and support, in particular, implementation of two of the innovations, specifically the CCSS and APPR (see Chapter 6 for more on the third innovation, DDI.)

Key differences between the odds-beating and typically performing schools lay in the ways transparent and reciprocal communications:

- Set the stage for change by offering clarity about what the innovations were, how they were to be implemented, in what time-frame, and by whom,
- Utilized open and diverse communication channels,
- Provided opportunities for multiway flow of ideas,
- Made use of "opportunity discourse" to mitigate stress associated with change, and
- Contributed to family and community support for innovation.

These features of communications contributed to the odds-beating schools' readiness to successfully implement the innovations and contributed to alignment across districts and schools, discussed in more detail in Chapter 5.

The following sections describe each of these features and provide representative examples drawn from the elementary and middle schools studied. This chapter concludes with a representative case in point from an odds-beating middle school where these five features of communications come to life.

Communicating to Set the Stage for Change

Proactive leaders examine internal and external political, economic, and societal environments and use what they learn to make decisions about organizational goals, resource allocations, and capacity. Many researchers have found that proactive leadership overall helps to account for innovation adoption and implementation readiness and capacity (Fixsen, Naoom, Friedman, & Wallace, 2005; Heifetz, 2006; Heifetz, Grashow, & Linsky, 2009; Malen et al., 2015; Weiner, 2009).

Evidence from this study shows a distinct difference in the proactive way that leaders in the odds-beating schools used communications to set the stage for the implementation of the standards and performance reviews. Leaders of both school and district provided clear and consistent messages to faculty about their own understandings of the purpose of the innovations and the organizational changes that implementing them would entail. Effective communications, in short, provided mutual clarity (DuFour & Fullan, 2013), especially with regard to how strictly teachers using state-recommended curriculum modules had to follow them.

District leaders in eleven of the twelve odds-beating schools (six elementary and five middle schools) were proactive in planning to adopt and implement the innovations prior to the mandate from the state. A major part of planning for the implementation of these innovations included three ways of discussing how the district would implement them. Discussions included:

- conversations with key stakeholders,
- district-wide communications to set expectations and goals for implementation, and
- the use of collaborative language that described the district as a team working together to implement the innovations for the benefit of all students.

Illustrations of this odds-beating characteristic come from both middle and elementary schools. For example, when leaders of Julesberg MS first began thinking about implementing the Common Core standards throughout the district, they began discussing it publicly in board of education meetings. These monthly conversations set the stage for defining the need for resources, parental support, and professional development. An assistant superintendent characterized these discussions as a strength of their implementation process.

When developing curriculum and instruction designed to meet the standards, Julesberg leaders established "network teams" to be the first to learn more from the state education department about what would be required so that they could share that information throughout the district. An assistant superintendent described how this process gave them a head start:

> If you look at the history of the Common Core standards, how districts were able to incorporate them into a change directive [to] learning and understanding, we very much were able to turn that around quite quickly, because . . . by the time a number of districts were just getting the training, our teachers had already received a number of materials. So I feel the network teams . . . helped this district put together a strong foundation.

District leaders for Julesberg continued to rely on open communications and collaboration to make decisions about implementing the Common Core standards as well as the new evaluation system. The superintendent described this as making people "anxious to contribute" to the success of the school and district. An assistant superintendent explained that when they were implementing the standards, they researched curricula and decided what to use on the basis of a committee of district and school leaders, teachers, and parents.

Additionally, based on teacher feedback, they also used grants to provide professional development for teachers in the use of new curricula in math and English language arts and in the use of data-driven instruction. Over the course of three years, they assessed student needs and applied to the state education department to slow the pace of math examinations and provide students with more supports.

In developing their APPR plan, Julesberg leaders also started ahead of the state's timetable. Based on committees and research, they concluded that they needed a good classroom observation tool and adopted the Danielson Framework for Teaching Evaluation Instrument (Danielson, 2011). Later, when they rolled out the APPR, they did so with the benefit of this model. They also proceeded slowly and provided professional development for everyone on the core features of using the Danielson rubrics.

Implementation of the Common Core standards proceeded similarly in the districts of all six odds-beating elementary schools. Planning was proactive and began well before the state-mandated implementation timeline. For example, a year in advance of the state's mandated implementation, the superintendent of Eagle Bluff ES set up curriculum teams to align curriculum district-wide to the new standards.

In odds-beating Spring Creek ES, the superintendent described Common Core implementation as "a huge change" for the district. As such, teams of instructional leaders and teachers began discussing and working together on implementing the changes early in order to take their time with implementation and get stakeholder feedback. In Starling Springs ES, the superintendent reported,

> We were doing those standards before they were called the Common Core. . . .
> We just didn't know it was Common Core then. We made the shift long before
> many districts I think [in] the region and the state did, because we already talked
> about doing that kind of work.

In contrast, district leaders of the typically performing schools were generally reactive to the state's requirements. District leaders of all the typically performing schools, both middle and elementary, reported that their implementation of the new requirements was made during the year in which they were mandated.

Open and Diverse Communication Channels

The communications channels in the odds-beating schools were multidirectional, clear, open, and available to professionals within the system. They were both formal (formal meetings, memos, strategic planning sessions) and informal (hallway communications, before- and after-school ad hoc meetings).

In addition, the forms of communication were multiple (e.g., e-mails, memos, grade portals, phone, and in-person conversations) across the district, within the school, and with community partners and parents. Another key factor in the open communications channels is the reciprocity – two-way conversations (both talking and listening) when leaders collaborate with teachers and others to gather information before making decisions.

At Yellow Valley ES, for example, regular faculty meetings are information sessions for all school staff. Additionally, in Eagle Bluff and Spring Creek, both rural elementary schools, the small size of the district and schools themselves encourages frequent informal communication among staff and school leaders. At Eagle Bluff, district leaders reported, and school staff concurred, that they make a point to be present in school buildings on a regular basis, furthering both formal and informal communication.

When asked about qualities of effective leadership, district leaders of odds-beating schools spoke about the importance of fostering effective communication channels. For example, in Bay City ES, a district administrator reported:

> We've really moved in this district beyond the administrator [principal] being the manager of the building. Of course you know there's always going to be managerial tasks, and I have to deal with those with them, but mostly to have those instructional conversations about what they're doing, what they need to do, how they're providing feedback, how they're providing staff development, how they're monitoring, and how I see it. . . . We have a lot of dialogue, a lot of conversations around data, around facts, around, "What are you doing, and what are you going to do?"

A district leader for Starling Springs ES echoed similar feelings about the importance of developing and sustaining effective and various communication channels:

> Leadership is really about a few things in my opinion. It's about communication. It's about relationship building, and it's also about following through on clear actions or goals, or both, so all those things are intertwined. The communication could be . . . all aspects of communication . . . meeting with one person, talking to a group, e-mail, social media, . . . large group meetings, and everywhere in between. But being a strong and consistent communicator I think is important for a leader.

The superintendent for Julesberg MS established expectations for open district-wide communication by creating a system of communication opportunities:

> We do [communication] formally and informally. Formally, it's one of the first things put on the table, when I meet everybody at the very first day. Every time you go to my website, you will see messages from me that emphasize the same thing whether it talks about schools, or the value of diversity—diversity of opinions, not just diversity in every other form. There are many formal

mechanisms, both technological and in terms of presentations and formal meetings.

Informally, I like to convey that what I like to do is to be as visible as possible, and as energetic as possible. . . . All of my meetings rotate in different buildings. So all of the principals have to meet with the supervisors; they must go to other buildings and have them host the building. In practice, it allows me to have dozens of extra informal connections that I wouldn't have if everybody keeps coming to me. I think there are signs of more and more collaboration and confidence in giving input because of [this].

Communication and Collaboration

Isolation is the enemy of improvement (Elmore, 2004), so communication and collaboration always matter, especially in times of turbulence and change. In the schools studied, collaborative efforts were aligned with and appeared to have built trust in the schools. As discussed in Chapter 2, relational trust in schools and districts (Bryk & Schneider, 2002) requires a symbiotic relationship with consistent interactions among the leaders, teachers, and others.

Conduits for these interactions are facilitated by clear goals and prioritization of collaboration to achieve those goals. Collaborative actions and their district-wide support in schools and districts can further cement trusting relationship and lead to improved performance in organizations (Bryk, Sebring, Allensworth, Luppescu, & Easton, 2010).

The twelve odds-beating schools showed evidence of consistent, enduring, and positive collaborative efforts among adults throughout the system. Of course, not every adult collaborated with every other adult. But, overall, in the odds-beating schools, teachers spoke of collaborating with each other and building leaders, building leaders described collaborating with district staff, and district staff collaborated with each other and with school staff. As shown in Figure 3.1, efforts to use communications to foster a culture of collaboration were deliberate in the odds beaters.

This collaboration was facilitated through communication of shared goals as well as clear signals that collaboration was a district-wide priority as demonstrated by allocation of time and resources. Throughout the odds-beating schools, district and school leaders communicated their continued support of collaborative efforts by reorganizing schedules and common planning times to allow teachers time and space to work together. Educators in the odds beaters generally spoke of a culture of collaboration that pervaded both district and school levels.

Further, educators discussed the importance of bidirectional communication regarding collaboration and goal setting. In other words, the work of

Culture and Communication

- Leadership, Leadership, Leadership – open, honest, transparent, approachable with strong follow through
- Collaborative, Consistent and Continual
- "Borish Redundancy"
- **One on one meetings** with teachers and attend grade level meetings
- Blog posts, newsletter, emails, BOCES staff development opportunities
- Parent and Community Evening Forums

Figure 3.1.   Poster from Spring Creek Elementary School District Office

creating and prioritizing time and resources for collaboration was in itself a collaborative effort where district and school leaders took into account feedback from teachers. This established a district-wide culture of collaboration for the odds-beating schools studied.

For example, in the elementary schools, common planning time was scheduled and used for its intended purpose. At Starling Springs, teachers use a professional learning community approach and focus their work on analyzing data and student work and developing plans for instruction. In Bay City and Yellow Valley, teachers have scheduled weekly grade-level common planning time, and this time is dedicated to discussions around instruction and student needs.

A Bay City ES instructional coach explained the essence of collaboration in her district:

> When I think of the culture of Bay City, I think of a whole group working together. It's such a group effort here. We have a very good support system. We all work together, just with different support systems. . . . I think how we work together is what makes it work. It comes from central office, where they know every building is different. Every building has different needs. . . . They listen, listen to what we need. As far as the leadership goes in this building, it is one of mutual respect. Everyone has a different job to do, and I think everyone can speak freely about what they need, what are their problems.

These differences between odds beaters and typical performers in terms of collaboration were also reflected in responses to an instructional survey administered in tandem with the site visit to each school. Reponses were suggestive of trends in communication and collaboration across schools. For example, teachers from odds-beating elementary schools were more likely than their peers in typical performers to report discussing at least once a week how to teach a topic (75% compared to 59%) and to share their learning experiences (70% compared to 59%).

They also reported being more likely to interact with their colleagues on four or more instructionally related topics at least once a week compared to their peers in typically performing schools. These results suggest that teachers in odds-beating schools tended to be somewhat more likely to interact at least weekly around instruction and learning how to teach than their peers in typically performing schools.

Similarly, leaders of the middle schools communicated their support for collaboration by not only talking about it but also creating time and resources to support collaborative efforts. For example, the principal of Sage City reported using time on teams to allow teachers to collaborate on curricular and instructional planning, discuss student data, and plan for other student needs.

She described a school culture in which leaders and teachers work together to create a "positive place," with time and materials to do the needed work and the understanding that the work takes time and support. Teachers also described a collaborative atmosphere with time for professional development, collaborative curricular development, and the freedom to ask for more resources if they need them. One teacher recounted the process of setting goals and working this way:

> I would say it's top down and bottom up. So . . . top down, from administration to us, the front line teachers, but also bottom up, because we do have teaming; we create goals and set objectives at a lower level as teams, with our chairperson, or even our cohorts, say within the grade that I teach, so all grade-level teachers are setting goals together.

In another example, district leaders for Laribee MS reconfigured team times to allow for collaborative work on developing standards-aligned instruction, provided funding and time for professional development to meet teacher and school leader needs, and distributed goal setting and other leadership activities throughout the district. A Laribee assistant superintendent described not only the way district leaders work closely together to make decisions but also how across the district multiple groups and committees consisting of teacher leaders, school leaders, and parent councils play various roles in decision making.

The principal of Laribee further described the school's collaborative efforts when discussing how the educators in the school had developed and implemented the district's action plan. Teachers and school staff corroborated they had received support from district leadership for their implementation of the standards in the classroom through professional development, shifting of finances to get needed resources, and the collaborative nature of the district in both deciding on and meeting goals.

Opportunity Discourse

Educators in the odds-beating schools in this study talked differently about change; the tone of discourse was distinctly different from that in typically performing schools. In the odds-beating schools, educators spoke of change in a positive way.

Leaders, in particular, chose to look at the mandated reforms as an opportunity. They set the stage for the innovations by acknowledging that they would be a challenge and require a new way of doing things, but they chose to promote the opportunities that implementing them would provide for teaching and learning. This type of "opportunity discourse" allowed leaders to create a system of learners—from leaders to teachers to students—where all embrace the idea of "getting better at getting better" (Bryk, Gomex, Grunow, & LeMahieu, 2015).

As noted earlier, this discourse started early in the process. Proactively communicating about the innovations and what they would require set a stage that allowed all leaders, teachers, staff, and parents to understand the innovations and accept the process. Throughout the long process of planning for and establishing the standards and implementing a new APPR plan, conversations continued. District leaders not only continued to recognize the challenges involved for the entire system, but they also emphasized that they knew that the district could meet and overcome those challenges.

The tone or "the way we talk" was particularly clear when school and district leaders and school staff discussed resources and student populations. First, in all eighteen schools and districts in this study, educators reported a perceived district-wide decline in resources for many reasons, including tax caps, the decline in the overall economy, reductions in personnel, and declining student enrollments.

However, in the twelve odds-beating schools, educators discussed resources in a way that was clearly more about opportunities and solutions than problems. In contrast, it was more common in typically performing schools for educators to report that declines in resources were sources of constraint. The positive tone that educators in odds beaters used to describe their ability to overcome challenges to implementation is referred to here as "opportunity discourse."

Drawing on findings from the odds-beating elementary schools in this study, examples demonstrate how the leaders in these schools and their district offices facilitated implementation of the CCSS and new APPR through opportunity discourse. This discourse helped build a climate of trust among educators, who often spoke of being "in this together, like a family."

In all six odds-beating elementary schools, the general sense was that, while they were facing challenges when it came to resources, they would pull together and find a way to meet the challenges. Leaders in their districts described planning early and collaboratively and involving school leaders in making resource decisions. For example, a Yellow Valley district leader said,

> I meet with every program manager—every principal, every department head, every director—in November. I start the budget early. So I schedule them to come in. They have last year's budget and then we have a clean slate and my assistant sits with her laptop and we go through every line item. . . . I always say to them, "Think about what your plan is for next year. We know we're going to do this with literacy. These are the costs I came up with. Is there anything else you need or you think you want to do with your staff next year?"
>
> . . . I let them come to the table with their ideas and then I build the budget from that. Also, in every department I give them the opportunity—we don't increase the budget at the building level—but I'll say, "This is what we have on paper, this is what you budgeted for last year. This is what you spent. You didn't spend this line. Do you want to shift that into a professional development line, or is there something you need to buy for your building?" That's how I build the budget. They have all the flexibility they want. They can make those decisions.

In Starling Springs, a district leader explained how the process of allocating resources is designed to protect student needs and district goals:

> We had to reduce by about $6 million in about a $113 million budget. So that's pretty significant, and there was really no way to do it other than somewhat across the board. . . . We try to really protect the classroom experience for kids . . . for the high school it was maybe cutting sections but not cutting course offerings and [at the] elementary level it may be not cutting class sizes . . . we try to protect all of those things. But at that level cuts needed to be made across the board, and so we still had to reduce in basically every area. But we tried.
>
> At least in my head what I always kind of thought was . . . if I were a 10-year-old, would I walk into school and notice a huge difference? But most 10-year-olds, or 16-year-olds in the high school for that matter, would not notice. The adults will be noticing, I think. . . . We cannot completely hide the reductions, but I think most of our students will not

see an enormous difference, which we feel pretty good about. So that was probably one of our guiding rationales. At the elementary levels, we wanted to protect some of our needier schools, too.

Additionally, leaders in odds-beating schools and their districts described alternative ways of finding the resources to meet student needs and goals, including working with community partners, applying for grants, restructuring roles of staff, and closely reviewing budgets and needs. Building-level leaders echoed that using resources wisely in an effort to meet goals was a top priority.

A leader at Eagle Bluff, for example, spoke of using resources within the school to meet the myriad needs of their special education students. Similarly, leaders at Spring Creek spoke of using in-house resources for special education students whenever possible, rather than sending them out to other programs (e.g., those offered by regional educational agencies).

In contrast, educators in the typically performing schools often used the language of constraints and barriers when it came to dealing with resource allocation decisions. For example, at Wolf Creek, teachers spoke resignedly of large class sizes and cuts that impacted technology. In Paige City, teachers and school leaders agreed that resource reallocations were cutting into professional development, common planning times, and levels of personnel. For example, the school had only one counselor for more than 600 students, and multiple people used the phrase "stretched too thin" to describe their work loads.

Another example of the use of opportunity discourse was displayed in the way educators in odds-beating schools discussed the populations they serve. All eighteen schools in this study have relatively challenging demographics. In 2012, all but one had greater than 17% of students from economically disadvantaged families; nine schools (six odds beaters and two typical performers) had greater than 40%.

Despite this poverty, educators in odds-beating schools tended to talk about their students, their communities, and students' families in positive terms, while educators at typically performing schools spoke more of the challenges they posed. For example, a Bay City district administrator, expressing a positive and proactive discourse, explained how their high-poverty population helps them provide additional services.

I'd like to say we have used our poverty wisely, or to the best that we could. It sounds like a little opposite statement, but when you think about it, we were allowed to—because of our poverty—to apply for and receive . . . many grants which helped us in presenting additional programs and services for kids that we knew that they needed, as well as our staff to be retrained or trained in the new kinds of students sitting before them in new numbers.

Constructive, Two-Way Communications with Parents

Transparent, two-way communications between educators and parents have been found to be central to parent engagement that impacts student achievement (e.g., Henderson, Mapp, Johnson, & Davies, 2007; Wilcox & Angelis, 2011). In the odds-beating schools, in general, communications were comparatively more consistent, more transparent (e.g., robust websites and e-mail), and more reciprocal (e.g., person to person) than in the typically performing schools. District and school leaders, teachers, and staffs promoted constructive, two-way communication with parents. As an assistant principal of Hutch Hill MS stated,

> Our website has evolved over the last couple of years to be a wealth of information. . . . We have blogs set up by our guidance department. Our faculty and staff utilize at least one method of communication . . . to text students and parents directly, to their websites, to their voicemail. . . . And we've realized that when all else fails, we just want you to pick up the phone and call us, or come in and meet.
>
> And even though we have all these other mechanisms in place, I think we do a very nice job of just being open and inviting to parents and to students if they want, if they have a question or if they have a concern, and they don't want to scour the website or look at a mobile app; they want that customer service—like when you're calling to find something that's wrong with your credit card or whatever, you want to talk to somebody. And I think parents feel comfortable coming into this building. I think we have a lot of different avenues for communication with parents.

While websites and e-mail have become the common strategies to inform parents of school programs, they do not necessarily encourage two-way communication. As the assistant principal of Hutch Hill implied, parents often wish to communicate with educators in person. Therefore, he believed that it was important for the school to be open and inviting to parents. Similar statements about the value of face-to-face interactions were lacking in typically performing schools. Instead, when asked about communicating with parents, responses were more like this one from a special education teacher at Tarelton MS:

> People seem to have email. It's easy for me at the end of the day to sit in my seat and report to this parent and that parent what's going on, what's happened. . . . Email is my saving grace because I'm busy, they're busy, and everyone seems to check their email.

In odds-beating schools, face-to-face communication was consistent with the schools' priority to overcome barriers to the basic necessity to effective communication: language. In Julesberg MS, for example, translators play a prominent role in supporting communication with linguistically diverse parents. According to an assistant principal, the translators "come to help set up parent meetings; they're invited in. We coordinate that service, so parents see that we are not just tuning them out because they don't speak English." Such culturally responsive approaches to students and families are discussed in more detail in Chapter 7.

Also, the substance of the communication differed between odds beaters and typical performers. In some of the odds-beating schools, educators reported using two-way communications with parents and the community to facilitate collaboration and shared decision making, as well as to provide (sometimes hands-on) opportunities to understand the Common Core standards and related shifts in curriculum, instruction, and assessment, as well as new evaluation systems for teachers and principals.

In Julesberg MS, for example, a district goal for 2014–15 was to strengthen communication with parents and community residents, and the reason given was to increase understanding of instructional programs and school district activities and initiatives. To that end, the district provided parent workshops presented by principals and teachers. The hands-on workshops were designed to help parents learn how to help their children learn and deepen their understanding of the standards. As described by the assistant superintendent, in these workshops,

> Parents have opportunities to be students—work with using informational text, use the mathematic practices. So that is an opportunity to experience school as their children experience school, and then turn around and talk about how they could support [the work] at home.

Educators in Starling Spring ES provided similar opportunities for parents and attributed the community's general support for the required changes on communications with parents and parents' understanding of the intent of the standards: fostering higher levels of thinking and student engagement.

Although educators at typically performing Silver City MS also tried to engage parents in understanding the innovations and used a translator in that effort, results were different. As a district leader described it:

> [The school has] a curriculum night . . . not an open house but a night we are really going to talk about what kids are learning, and we really wanted a student, a parent to be there. We reached out a couple of times and we really didn't get anything back, which can happen with these families. We engaged a phone call with a translator, and we translated a letter to the family, and they still didn't come. But we do our best.

Even though Silver City used the service of a translator in communicating with parents, it is evident that at Julesberg the translator was an integral part of establishing contact and interacting with parents rather than merely serving as a contracted translation service.

In the odds-beating schools, parents' understanding of the overall goals of the standards were brought about, in part, through educator's efforts to communicate those goals and the innovations that would help achieve them. In some sites, it was communications that helped ease parents' initial frustration with the new curricula and instructional practices.

A CASE IN POINT—HUTCH HILL MIDDLE SCHOOL

That is why we are all here—we are all here to support that classroom. To support the teacher and to support the kids in that classroom. That's where it counts, so I think that message is loud and clear in our district.

—deputy superintendent

District leaders of Hutch Hill Middle School emphasized frequent and clear communications to establish system-wide trust, the district vision and mission, and use of organizational redesign elements to facilitate and assist in the implementation of the Common Core standards and new APPR system. The deputy superintendent described a district where everyone is valuable and important and contributes to the education of children in the classroom, stating,

> We pay a lot of attention to teachers. My message, as consistently as I can give it, is we're all important. Bus drivers are important, cafeteria people are important, administrators are important, everybody is important. But there is nobody more important than the classroom teacher.

To that end, she emphasized the importance of several things to support teachers and school leaders. First, she reported facilitating a positive climate where everyone feels valued and positive about their roles in the district. Second, she stated, "We place a lot of emphasis on professional development. We give teachers what they need in terms of PD." Third, she reported an important level of professional learning community work happening throughout the district, which aligned instructional, curricular, social-emotional, and other goals for students.

Interviews and focus groups with middle school leaders and faculty indicated that these leadership strategies were part of the district culture of supporting the instructional core of teaching and learning. Teachers and school leaders reported that they understood the goals of meeting student needs both in the classroom and beyond, goals that are set through collaborative processes. As described by the principal, "The things that we've come up with in the building as targets that . . . [district leaders] have entrusted us with—that's the work that needs to be done in order to achieve those district goals."

District leaders were proactive in anticipating the advent of the Common Core standards and beginning the work early and proceeding through implementation with the support of the board of education, professional development, collaborative goal setting, and professional learning communities within the schools. The deputy superintendent described the importance of including teacher leaders in implementing new practices:

> It's really that we value our grade-level leaders and our department chairs. I know that our building principals rely on them heavily. They have lots of meetings, lots of discussions, and big decisions are made in collaboration with teachers. They are the ones that . . . have the great information about what will work or what won't work, and we have people who just take the ball and run with it. We almost sometimes can't keep up with all of them. But it's really great and anything that we've done that's worked well has been teacher led.

Middle school leaders agreed that they had begun the processes of implementing the standards early. The principal described having a certain level of autonomy to meet with the professional learning communities (PLCs) and create curriculum strategies, collaborate around Common Core applications and assessments, and embed professional development, all with district support.

In Hutch Hill, trust is evident throughout the district in the many forms of communication from the district to the school staff; in the autonomy given to teachers to provide expertise both in the classroom and in planning and development meetings; and in the system-wide clarity and coherence of goals, vision, and mission of the district.

As the superintendent reported, "It has to do with climate and atmosphere, but it's trust. There's a high level of trust between the teachers and . . . between everybody in the district." District leaders reported high levels of trust with teachers and other school-level staff, the board of education, and families. Teachers and school leaders agreed and reported working closely both with each other and district leaders to create a trusting and collaborative system (Hutch Hill Case in Point from Wilcox et al., 2015).

SUMMARY

There was a clear difference between odds-beating and typically performing schools in this study in their actions, language, and practices of using communications to support implementation of innovations. In the odds beaters, district and school leaders used communication effectively to set the stage and tone for adopting and implementing the Common Core standards and new APPR system. Communication was used in multiple ways and through a myriad of pathways to build district-wide collaborative efforts.

Educators described the importance of getting timely, clear information and having ways to provide that same information to other educators, parents, and community members. Equally as critical was the sense that the language used was opportunity based and focused on meeting and surpassing challenges as a team.

All in all, leaders of odds-beating schools and their districts used effective communications mechanisms to prepare educators for the innovations and support them as they learned new ways of teaching. Communications across the odds beaters were clear and reciprocal, employed multiple channels, and included families. In addition, the tone of communications acknowledged challenges but presented the challenges as an opportunity to improve teaching and learning. Ultimately, this opportunity discourse was a framework for facilitation of change

REFERENCES

Bryk, A.S., Gomez, L.M., Grunow, A., & LeMahieu, P.G. (2015) *Learning to improve: How America's schools can get better at getting better*. Boston, MA: Harvard Education Press.

Bryk, A.S., Sebring, P., Allensworth, E., Luppescu, S., & Easton, J. (2010). *Organizing schools for improvement: Lessons from Chicago*. Chicago: University of Chicago Press.

Bryk, A.S., & Schneider, B. (2002). *Trust in schools: A core resource for improvement*. New York: Russell Sage Foundation.

Danielson, C. (2011). The 2011 teaching evaluation instrument. The Danielson Group. Downloaded from: https://www.danielsongroup.org/books-materials/

Datnow, A. (2006). Connections in the policy chain: The "co-construction" of implementation in comprehensive school reform. In M.I. Honig (Ed.), *New directions in education policy implementation: Confronting complexity* (pp. 105–124). Albany, NY: State University of New York Press.

DuFour, R., & Fullan, M. (2013). *Cultures built to last: Systemic PLCs at work*. Bloomington, IN: Solution Tree Press.

Durand, F.T., Lawson, H.A., Wilcox, K.C., & Schiller, K.S. (2016). The role of district office leadership in the adoption and implementation of the Common Core State Standards in elementary schools. *Educational Administration Quarterly*, 51(1), 45–74. doi:10.1177/0013161x15615391

Elmore, R. (2004). *School reform from the inside out: Policy, practice, and performance*. Cambridge, MA: Harvard Education Press.

Fixsen, D.L., Naoom, S., Blase, K., Friedman, R., & Wallace, F. (2005). *Implementation research: A synthesis of the literature.* Tampa, FL: Louis de la Parte Florida Mental Health Research Institute, University of South Florida. http://nirn.fpg.unc.edu/sites/nirn.fpg.unc.edu/files/resources/NIRN-MonographFull-01-2005.pdf.

Fullan, M. (2001). *Leading in a culture of change.* San Francisco: Jossey-Bass.

Fullan, M. (2006). *Turnaround leadership.* San Francisco: Jossey-Bass, Wiley Imprint.

Heifetz, R.A. (2006). Anchoring leadership in the work of adaptive process. In F. Hesselbein & M. Goldsmith (Eds.), *The leader of the future 2: Visions, strategies, and practices for a new era* (pp. 73–84). San Francisco: Jossey-Bass, Wiley Imprint.

Heifetz, R., Grashow, A. & Linsky, M. (2009). *The practice of adaptive leadership: Tools and tactics for changing your organization and the world.* Boston, MA: Harvard Business Press.

Henderson, A.T., Mapp, K, Johnson, V., & Davies, D. (2007). *Beyond the bake sale: The essential guide to family-school partnerships.* New York: The New Press.

Honig, M.I. (2004). Where's the "up" in bottom-up reform? *Educational Policy,* 18(4), 527–561.

Honig, M.I. (2014). Beyond the policy memo: Designing to strengthen the practice of district central office leadership for instructional improvement at scale. In B.J. Fishman, W.R. Penuel, A.R. Allen, & B.H. Cheng (Eds). *Design-based implementation research.* National Society for the Study of Education Yearbook, 112(1).

Honig, M.I., & Copland, M.A. (2014). Conditions supportive of central office leadership for instructional improvement. In M.S. Knapp, M. Honig, M. Plecki, B. Portin, & M. Copland (Eds.), *Learning-focused leadership in action: Improving instruction in schools and districts* (pp. 102–120). New York: Routledge.

Knapp, M.S., Honig, M.I., Plecki, M., Portin, B., & Copland, M. (2014). *Learning-focused leadership in action: Improving instruction in schools and districts.* New York: Routledge.

Lawson, H.A., Durand, F.T, Wilcox, K.C., Gregory, K., Schiller K.S. & Zuckerman, S (2017). The role of district and school leaders' trust and communications in the simultaneous implementation of policy innovations. *Journal of School Leadership,* 27(1).

Leithwood, K., & Sun, J. (2012). The nature and effects of transformational school leadership: A meta-analytic review of unpublished research. *Educational Administration Quarterly,* 48(3), 387–423. doi: 10.1177/0013161X11436268

Malen, B., Rice, J., Matlach, L., Bowsher, A., Hoyer, K., & Hyde, L. (2015). Developing organizational capacity for implementing complex education reform initiatives: Insights from a multi-year study of a teacher incentive fund program. *Educational Administration Quarterly,* 51(1), 133–176. doi: 10.1177/0013161X14522482

Marzano, R.J. (2003). What works in schools: Translating research into action. Alexandria, VA: Association for Supervision and Curriculum Development.

Marzano, R.J. & Waters, T. (2009) *District leadership that works: Striking the right balance.* Bloomington, IN: Solution Tree.

Weiner, B. J. (2009). A theory of organizational readiness for change. *Implementation Science*, 4: 67. Open Access, Published 19 October 2009. doi:10.1186/1748-5908-4-67

Wilcox, K.C., & Angelis, J.I. (2011). *Best practices from high-performing high schools: How successful schools help students stay in school and thrive.* New York: Teachers College Press.

Wilcox, K.C., Durand, F.T., Gregory, K., Schiller, K.S., Lawson, H., Zuckerman, S., Felicia, N., & Angelis, J.I. (2015). *Odds-beating middle schools cross-case report.* Prepared for the New York State Education Department as part of the School Improvement Study. Albany, NY: State University of New York.

Chapter Four

Alignment and Coherence

Sarah J. Zuckerman, Hal A. Lawson, and Kristen Campbell Wilcox

Although the "what" of the three policy innovations—the Common Core State Standards, annual professional performance reviews based in part on student assessments, and data-driven instruction—was delineated by the state, the "how" of implementation was largely left up to local leaders to figure out. Inevitably, a myriad of "how" questions arose, particularly pertaining to implementation strategies that would fit local contexts and their associated adult learning and resource reallocation needs.

One weakness of the state's approach was that it did not take into account the variable competencies of district leaders to know how to achieve alignment and craft coherence across districts and schools while simultaneously implementing multiple innovations. Leaders of the odds-beating schools, however, managed the alignment and coherence challenges in qualitatively different ways than their peers in typically performing schools. These differences are the focus of this chapter.

One difference relates to the stance district leaders took toward schools. For example, superintendents of many of the typically performing schools in this study opted for relatively strict, compliance-oriented implementation strategies such as mandating faithful adoption of state-recommended curriculum modules (discussed in more detail in Chapter 6). In contrast, superintendents of the odds-beating schools chose strategies that encouraged professional discretion to meet well-defined goals.

Considering the improvement principle of crafting work in ways that are user-centered, that is, taking into account the points of view of a variety of stakeholders about what might—and might not—work in a particular setting (Bryk, Gomez, Grunow, & LeMahieu, 2015), these superintendents worked closely with their school boards, other district office leaders, principals, and teachers (including union leaders) as they collaboratively made sense of the innovations (Coburn & Russell, 2008). They then collaboratively developed implementation strategies deemed fit for purpose in their respective districts (Durand, Lawson, Wilcox, & Schiller, 2016).

The ability of district leaders to filter innovations through existing understandings appears to have been supported by two interrelated features: alignment and coherence (Daly & Finnigan, 2016). These features comprise the interorganizational structures and mechanisms for and interpersonal facilitators of acting and meaning making that support innovation implementation on the scale of school and district (DuFour & Fullan, 2013).

Together, alignment and coherence served as linchpins in cross-boundary systems change in the odds-beating schools (see Chapter 8). Three reminders foreground the ensuing discussion with regard to alignment and coherence:

- Districts and their constituent schools are understood to be complex, interrelated systems (Senge et al., 2012);
- Changes in one part of a complex system are expected to impact others; and
- The Common Core State Standards (CCSS), annual professional performance reviews (APPR), and data-driven instruction (DDI) are examples of system-changing innovations that were intended to penetrate to the instructional core.

In this systems change framework, rapid, dramatic innovation implementation creates daunting complexity and predictably results in uncertainty and emotional stress (Heifetz, Grashow, & Linsky, 2009). Especially when implemented simultaneously, the CCSS, APPR, and DDI are "disruptive innovations" (Christensen, Horn, & Johnson, 2011). Without attention to innovation implementation strategies for alignment and coherence, disruptive innovations can be expected to result in performance declines. To prevent such declines, ensuring alignment and coherence would seem essential corequisites for successful innovation implementation.

ALIGNMENT, COHERENCE, AND THEIR RELATIONSHIPS

Unfortunately, alignment and coherence tend to be conflated not only in everyday practice but also in textbooks and research journals. Although they surely are related, they refer to different phenomena, and it is possible to have one without the other. Both are needed during periods of rapid innovation implementation in district offices and constituent schools.

Alignment: Cross-Boundary Structures and Mechanisms

District central offices, constituent schools, and partner agencies that provide educational services (e.g., career and technical education and special education services) are, in one view, discrete organizations with their respective boundaries, role and relationship systems, cultures and climates, and facilities. When a systems change view is substituted for this stand-alone view, the need for commonalities and complementarities between schools and other entities within a district becomes evident.

Alignment is the concept used to identify, describe, and implement the cross-boundary structures and mechanisms that support these commonalities and complementarities. Structures and mechanisms for data collection and dissemination and resource allocation are two examples. These top-down and bottom-up structures and mechanisms are facilitated by a combination of trusting relationships and reciprocal communications, as detailed in Chapters 2 and 3 (Lawson et al., 2017).

Coherence: Educators' Shared Ideas and Understandings

Alignment structures and mechanisms support and facilitate coherence among individuals as they strive to meet goals (Grossman, Hammerness, McDonald, & Ronfeldt, 2008). When these structures and mechanisms connect multiple levels of the system, they provide opportunities for reciprocal communication. Reciprocal communication contributes to the development of shared ideas and understandings, which in turn build alignments in key areas such as instructional programming (Johnson, Marietta, Higgins, Mapp, & Grossman, 2015).

Such coherence is grounded in widespread clarity among educators regarding the content and purpose of change. Fullan and Quinn (2016) situate coherence in people: "When large numbers of people have a deeply understood sense of what needs to be done—and see their part in that purpose—coherence emerges and powerful things happen" (p.1). This requires a "shared depth of understanding about the purpose and nature of the work. Coherence, then, is what is in the minds and actions of people individually and, especially, collectively" (pp. 1–2).

Recent research describes the essential role that leaders play in organizational learning and in nurturing coherence within their organizations (e.g., Knapp, Honig, Plecki, Portin, & Copland, 2014; Simmons, 2006). Frameworks that provide strategies for crafting coherence highlight that leaders' work in this regard is never ending: Given the recent past, it is likely that schools will continue to experience disruptive innovations, raising questions as to how and why to approach them (Durand et al., 2016; Honig & Hatch, 2004).

Connecting Alignment and Coherence

Daly and Finnigan (2016) emphasize the collective, or relational, nature of coherence and alignment. They introduce the concept of relational coherence to underscore that coherence is not merely in the hearts and minds of individuals; rather it is a collective property necessary for alignments across systems. "Systemwide approaches require attention not just to all of the actors in the system, but also to the interconnectedness of the actors. . . . Attention to horizontal, vertical, and developmental coherence is important because it is often through these kinds of coherence that reform and change take place" (p. 236).

They also introduce the concept of relational alignment, which moves beyond the structures and mechanisms that provide connections within schools and between schools and districts to include the human interactions that animate alignment. In their words:

> Current reforms in education, which focus heavily on improving the technical core of the work, are important but will not be effective unless attention also is given to the ways in which trust, innovative climate, and systemwide learning come together. Without these relational alignments, improvement is unlikely (p. 236).

This ideal state of both relational coherence and relational alignment is not a one-time event or an easy achievement. Thus, the strategies used in odds-beating schools and districts to facilitate alignment and coherence should be of considerable interest to others. These strategies are described in the section that follows, with contrasting examples from the typical performers. The chapter closes with a case in point from an odds-beating elementary school that provides a more detailed example.

ALIGNMENT- AND COHERENCE-FACILITATING STRATEGIES IN THE ODDS BEATERS

Across the odds-beating schools, educators credited three common characteristics to fostering alignment and coherence:

- Clear articulation of a widely understood, collaboratively created vision and mission, combined with commonly understood, aligned measurable goals;

- Systematic processes for the continual revision of curriculum and associated instructional alignments within schools and across the district;
- Data systems that allow for course corrections when measured against district, school, and classroom goals.

Developing and Communicating a Clear Vision, Mission, and Goals

Educators in the majority of odds-beating schools were clear about their district and school vision and mission. They also described school and district goals that were well aligned to the vision and mission and how these goals drove processes and practices at multiple organizational levels. Teachers and district leaders explained how diverse stakeholders, ranging from school board members to teachers, had opportunities to contribute to the overall agenda, which created shared ownership and understanding.

Vision, Mission, and Goals and Relational Coherence

Teachers and support staff at the odds-beating schools expressed an awareness and understanding of the vision, mission, and goals set at the district level. For example, teachers at Bay City ES said, "Our district as a whole has a goal of test scores improving for ELA [English language arts] and math," and "Usually goals are through the data binders; a lot of our goals come from there."

Similarly, at Eagle Bluff ES, teachers and administrators spoke of "cascading goals" at the levels of district, school, and within content areas. Teachers and administrators identified both academics and an "outer circle" of social and emotional development to support academic achievement.

Middle school teachers and administrators also expressed an understanding of district-level vision and goals. For example, at Hutch Hill, district administrators, building leaders, teachers, and support staff described the vision and goals as organizing principles and the driving force for their work. They reported that district goals are included on all meeting agendas and that they drive decision making. For example, the principal explained,

> Essentially we have our mission statement and our core values that ultimately drive the decisions that we make districtwide. We're constantly communicating about things we're doing programmatically to make sure that we're on the same page.

In the same vein, the superintendent reported including the vision and mission in his presentations, saying, "Living the core values needs to be done."

In a number of odds-beating schools, teachers reported constant reminders of the vision and goals. For example, at Eagle Bluff ES and Ruby MS, when describing district goals, many teachers referenced printed vision and goal statements posted in their classrooms and conference rooms.

In contrast, none of the typically performing schools provided evidence of leaders and teachers having clear and consistent understandings of the district or school vision or mission. Reports of district and school goals often indicated misalignments between them. In some typically performing schools, district administrators articulated a vision, but it was not clearly aligned with other district administrators' understandings of the vision. Nor did it align well with the mission or goals.

For example, the superintendent of typically performing Locus Glen MS spoke about a set of "wildly important goals" and "filters for action" that drive decision making at the district level. However, at the building level, only the principal referenced either the goals or the filters for action and did so in a limited manner. And at the typically performing Wolf Creek ES, when asked about the vision for the school, one building leader responded, "The honest answer to that is I'm not sure of what the vision is."

At the typically performing Sun Hollow ES, the principal explained that a number of problems arise because of the absence of a clear, compelling, and collaboratively developed vision, mission, and goals, especially ones centered on what school staff understand as central to their work of teaching:

> The board of education has set forth subject-specific goals that in all honesty I don't remember. When I look at them and read them, they make sense. [But] they're not always directly aligned with where administration and the teachers want to go.

Collective Goal Setting, Widespread Ownership

The Sun Hollow principal's statement reflects a lack of collective attention to goal setting, which was common in the typical performers, where limited relational coherence district-wide was apparent. In contrast, educators in odds-beating schools described goal setting as a collaborative process that included input from a variety of stakeholders at multiple organizational levels, including school board members, district administrators, building leaders, and teachers.

For example, at Eagle Bluff ES, the principal, superintendent, and teachers described annual processes for collective goal setting beginning at the district and then moving to the building level. Similarly, at Starling Springs ES, a district leader reported the goal-setting process as ongoing and focused on learning and instruction, with "our big goals com[ing] really from our work with the school board."

Likewise, educators at the odds-beating middle schools reported collaborative goal setting at district and school levels. At Julesburg, the superintendent explained that "the goals the district designs and articulates are a product of a lot of conversations" between the school board and administrators. A site-based team of administrators and curriculum supervisors then align school goals with those developed by the board through these conversations. Teachers reported aligning their goals to those set by the school board.

At Roaring Gap MS, district and building leaders articulated how district goals become the "template" for building-level goals. The superintendent emphasized that linking district and school goals helped the district move from a "confederation of loosely coupled classrooms and schools" to a "comprehensive, cohesive school district."

In a similar vein, at Ruby MS, the superintendent reported shared decision-making processes on the part of teachers and the wider community in the development of the strategic plan to meet goals. The superintendent reported looking forward to "get[ting] another one rolling so we can start to envision where we're going next."

At Hutch Hill MS, a similar process engaged both the school board and teachers. The superintendent reported that goal setting begins with district office leaders and the school board and that the "field" (building leaders and teachers) "further develop those areas the board was interested in. . . . It came originally from the field to the board and then back to the field." He added that school board members "appreciate the fact that teachers are involved in developing the goals, because they know the goals are going to be carried out."

The collaborative processes at Hutch Hill reflect a sense of the importance of teacher ownership of and contribution to building-level goals. This emphasis on ownership was also observed at Eagle Bluff ES. The principal there reported that developing goals with teachers "makes our goals document that much more real, because it's ours. It isn't something I did, it wasn't something they did; it was something we did collaboratively."

Alignment of Instructional Systems

In addition to the development of coherence through collaborative generation of vision, mission, and goals, the odds-beating schools displayed higher degrees of agreement as to how to meet desired outcomes through alignment in the instructional system—curriculum, instructional practices, and assessments. This alignment was facilitated by structured and collaborative sensemaking activities, that is, ones that yield relational alignment. The result was high levels of agreement among teachers and leaders as to what constitutes quality classroom experiences for students.

Alignment of curriculum in several odds-beating schools proceeded through ongoing revision and evaluation activities, while alignment of instructional practices developed through common professional development and shared expectations. The differences between odds beaters and typical performers in this regard emerged as those of degree, not of absence or presence.

Reenvisioning the Curriculum

Curriculum alignment in the odds-beating schools proceeded largely through interactions between teachers and principals at the building level. At Julesburg MS, a teacher credited this work with helping "to make sense with a very difficult—I guess you'd say, turbulent—time in education." District leaders of these schools also spoke of purposefully engaging in vertical curriculum alignment across the district.

For example, at Roaring Gap MS, district leaders reported that the CCSS provided a pathway to implement their goal of a "defined, guaranteed curriculum." Further, administrators reported that the standards provided a structure for common units and assessments across both middle schools in the district. District content area directors described teachers working together to integrate the standards into the existing district curriculum and creating curriculum maps. These maps were made available to all teachers. The superintendent described such efforts as helping each school see their contribution to the district.

Similarly, at Eagle Bluff ES, a number of administrators and teachers identified collaboration between teachers at the three elementary schools and at the middle school as key to successful curriculum revisions. They identified this collaboration as facilitating alignment of the district's curriculum and ensuring that students from all three elementary schools arrived at the middle school with similar prior experiences. One district administrator described the work of teacher teams in grades 5–8 in aligning the mathematics curriculum and integrating the CCSS:

> The 5-8 congruency team in mathematics would take a look at three areas we focus on: curriculum, instruction, and assessment. They would take a look at the alignment of their curriculum across grades 5-8 with regards to the mathematics Common Core to make sure that whatever adjustments they might need to make to the curriculum are made, and also to create a plan to take them to fruition.

At Hutch Hill MS, teachers reported a similar collaborative approach. One stated, "When we come together and take all those Common Core alignments and the standards, I think it allows us to collaborate and create an even better curriculum." The principal emphasized the ongoing nature of this collaborative attention to curriculum revision, "It's an all-day, everyday conversation, and I think we're always looking—whether you're revamping a lesson from one year to the next, or you're revamping a lesson from first block, it's all about reflection and always looking to analyze your practice and student learning."

As discussed in Chapter 3, like the other odds beaters, at Hutch Hill, collaborative conversations about the Common Core began well in advance of the state-mandated implementation. Not only did those early conversations "soften the blow," as one teacher said, but, "Starting those conversations five years ago . . . we were able to foresee what was coming and work as a group to build the collective responsibility that we feel as a building that everyone is part of this."

While collaborative processes at the odds-beating schools contributed to the alignment of curriculum, they did not lead to lock-step implementation. Rather, teachers were given discretion to adapt the curriculum to meet student needs. For example, at Roaring Gap MS, one district content area director reported,

> I think that they [the teachers] do need flexibility and they do need to explore their own path of instruction. . . . I want them to have that flexibility, but standards are consistent and the core text is consistent and we have developed a calendared curriculum so that we know when different standards are going to be taught and assessed.

Likewise, teachers at Starling Springs ES reported working together to develop a shared curriculum map and integrating the new standards. The superintendent described flexibility for teachers within this aligned curriculum, reporting that he holds teachers "accountable for those key metrics," adding, "we've been very loose about what they use."

At other odds-beating schools, teachers also reported discretion within a structure of an aligned curriculum, particularly in adapting the state curriculum modules to meet the needs of their students. For example, teachers at Bay City ES reported making collective and collaborative decisions at their grade levels in implementing the modules for their students. Teachers at Yellow Valley ES also reported using the modules as a starting point to meet the needs of their students and the use of common planning time to develop lessons together.

However, at the typically performing schools, efforts to develop an aligned curriculum proceeded in a more top-down manner. Such implementation left little room for teacher collaboration or discretion in implementation. For example, at Sun Hollow ES, the principal and superintendent spoke of using the curriculum modules from the state as a means to leverage an aligned curriculum onto teachers.

And at Locus Glen MS, the superintendent cited the state's modules as offering a higher level of rigor than teacher-developed curriculum in his decision to mandate use of the modules. In response, English-language arts teachers reported a sense of loss of their literature-based curriculum and frustrations with the restraints of using the modules as a scripted program. One teacher stated, "Just one more among a litany of things to take control from us. I think it makes us feel devalued."

On the other hand, at Tarelton MS, a lack of collaboration and clearly defined expectations combined to create an uneven implementation of the new standards. Teachers reported freedom to use the state curriculum modules or to integrate the standards into the previous curriculum. Several noted their concerns that students coming from the elementary school had not been exposed to the same academic language. At Silver City MS, implementation of the new standards proceeded concurrently with other instructional and curriculum innovations, resulting in overload and a lack of clarity as to how all of the pieces come together in the classroom.

Alignment of Instructional Practices

The alignment of instructional practices throughout the odds-beating schools fell along a continuum. At one end was a negotiated shared instructional practice; at the other was a more flexible approach with a set of shared expectations. In contrast, the typically performing schools appeared to follow either of two other paths: They implemented a "too tight" approach (Fullan, 2006), with top-down mandates for strict module implementation fidelity; or they opted for a "too loose" approach (Fullan, 2006), with teachers acting autonomously, resulting in implementation of the CCSS unevenly across classrooms.

On the shared instructional practices end of the continuum, teachers in both odds-beating Ruby MS and Eagle Bluff ES employed similar instructional strategies, which teachers and administrators credited to shared professional development. At Eagle Bluff, a district leader described this professional development as creating alignment across the elementary schools so that students enter the middle school having seen "the same types of instructional strategies; the teachers are talking the same language."

Although Eagle Bluff teachers reported initial skepticism, one described the strategies as "really good." Another concurred, stating, "I use them all the time." A third teacher stated, "I think [that approach] is really effective for us because we have to make every minute count."

Observed examples of such instructional strategies in ELA and math classrooms included:

- the use of bell ringers to review skills prior to the start of the lesson,
- having students repeat task directions,
- providing think time for students and allowing partner and small group conversations prior to answering questions,
- the use of cold calls to keep students on their toes and engaged, and
- positive reinforcement.

Further along the continuum, teachers at Hutch Hill MS reported flexibility and instructional risk taking within a framework of shared understanding of expectations, with students' needs at the center of decision making. As one teacher explained, "We're going to adapt [the modules] to target those students that are struggling." The principal reported encouraging teachers to take instructional risks in the classroom, to try new things, and to learn together from looking at data in their professional learning communities.

At Sage City MS, teachers reported, "We share everything—what works, what doesn't, lessons, periodic benchmark assessments . . . [asking] 'Where are the gaps, how do we close those gaps?' . . . There's a lot of dialogue going on." At Bay City ES, teachers also enjoyed considerable discretion in instructional practices; however, teachers reported working together during their common planning time to reflect together on instruction.

In typically performing schools, practices fell into one of two extremes: Representing the "too loose" approach, teachers at Tarelton MS employed a wide range of instructional techniques in an environment with infrequent collaboration around instruction. As a result, Tarelton teachers and administrators expressed concern about students not being on the same page. And at Wolf Creek ES, garbled messages between district leaders and teachers diminished any sense of shared expectations about whether adaptation of mandated modules was permissible.

At the opposite extreme of top-down alignment of instructional practices, teachers at two of the typical performers expressed frustration at the local mandate to use the modules as a scripted instructional program. At Locus Glen MS, teachers reported that the modules were difficult to use without modification. One reported making extensive notes on a digital copy but found it difficult to use the plans in class because students did not respond as anticipated by the script. Teachers at Paige City ES expressed frustration at the "super-scripted" nature of the modules.

Professional Development for Instructional Alignment

All systems changes and innovation implementation initiatives depend on adult learning (Hall & Hord, 2006; Senge et al., 2012), which means that professional development is essential to achieving relational coherence and relational alignment. Resources, then, need to be allocated accordingly.

In the odds-beating schools, developing a shared sense of curriculum and instruction appeared to be aided by professional development activities aligned to district and school priorities. At several schools, leaders provided significant professional development on the new standards well ahead of the state's implementation timeline. This gave teachers an extended timeline to develop an understanding of the standards and integrate them into their curriculum and instruction.

For example, at Julesburg MS, administrators and teachers reported using state-provided turnkey training on the Common Core standards as early as 2010, three years prior to the state mandate. One district administrator credited such proactive professional development for the school's success, feeling that, in comparison to nearby districts, Julesberg "teachers were better trained and had advanced knowledge."

Some districts hired outside consultants to provide the professional development. An administrator at Goliad ES reported that the external trainer was able to provide a depth of knowledge for teachers that was deeper than what a "[local service agency] could have done." At Bay City ES, district administrators contracted with an external consultant on an ongoing basis to provide training on the CCSS to teachers and on classroom observation skills for principals.

At Spring Creek ES, the district was investing in professional development aligned to the state curriculum modules, as well as Singapore Math, found by many schools to align well with the CCSS. One teacher reported that the district makes good use of staff development days to align instruction: "Our staff development days are geared towards helping us, instructionally, in the classroom. They really are power packed. They are not just days on the calendar."

In the typically performing schools, less proactive approaches to providing professional development around the innovations were evident. At Wolf Creek ES, one teacher stated, "It was training and teaching it at one time. There was one day of math in the summer. For ELA, we had an afternoon before we started." At Locus Glen MS, teachers reported a last-minute decision to adopt the modules, and although the district provided some training during the first year of implementation, it was seen by teachers as having limited utility. At Sun Hollow ES, teachers and principals reported limited professional development opportunities.

In addition to providing training aligned specifically to the standards and state modules, leaders of odds-beating schools tended to provide additional professional development aligned to their own goals. For example, the commitment to strengthen literacy instruction at Yellow Valley ES was matched by ongoing training for literacy coaches who support classroom teachers as well as a focus on working with students in poverty. A district official reported that the funds for this professional development came out of the general budget, and although it was expensive, the results justified the expenditure.

As mentioned earlier, teachers at Eagle Bluff ES received common professional development in instructional strategies. District and school leaders indicated that they allocate funds for this professional development activity every year. An assistant superintendent credited it with providing a source of coherence and consistency throughout the district: "[It] provides a common platform, a common terminology, and a common way of instructing across the district. So as students come up through each elementary and when they get to the middle school, they see the same types of instructional strategies."

At Hutch Hill a district leader reported that even when teachers are allowed discretion in their professional development activities, they are expected to align with district priorities:

> The professional development helps a lot in terms of consistency. And we don't allow teachers to go willy-nilly wherever they want to. . . . It has to fit within more globally our mission statement/core values, and then within the district goals. It's got to address a district goal, whatever workshops they may go to.

And he continued, "We don't have a lot of teachers going to workshops because we provide a lot of professional development right here on campus."

In the odds-beating schools, such locally developed professional development complements external opportunities and may be provided by building leaders. The assistant principal at Hutch Hill gave an example: "There's constant professional development on how to best deliver instruction. . . . For instance, at the next building meeting [the principal] will take everybody through how to do a read-aloud type of activity, a structured read-aloud."

At Laribee MS as the assistant principal described working with the principal around project-based learning and differentiated instruction, two of the goals of the middle school. District and school leaders reported that professional development offerings were determined, in part, by conversations among content specialists, the principal, and teachers. Such internal professional development often reflected collaborative practices that contributed to relational coherence.

Similarly, at Sage City MS, the assistant principal reported working with the principal and the department heads together as a group or in team meetings on professional development days. Teachers added that offerings on professional development days may be run by teachers, assistant superintendents, or outside individuals. Likewise, at Yellow Valley ES, teachers attend professional development during two faculty meetings a month and district-wide grade-level meetings once a month. At Bay City ES, teachers reported monthly early release time to examine student work samples together.

At Roaring Gap MS, full-time content area coaches work in an embedded professional development model with teachers. The superintendent described these positions as working "hand-in-hand with teachers—coteaching lessons and coplanning—not just helping teachers understand, but also modeling and getting feedback in a collegial basis for what the Common Core looks like." These coaches reported working collaboratively with their grade-level teams around classroom instruction and using data.

On the other hand, the typically performing schools revealed limited input from teachers and principals in regard to needed professional development. The Silver City MS principal reported that in the past the district had tended to offer the same professional development opportunities every year, adding, "I asked for some PD for people around developing Common Core formative assessments and the development of rubrics." However, the district did not provide it. The assistant principal noted that the district is a major source of professional development, particularly in regard to the district's many programmatic initiatives.

Using Data Systems to Foster Alignment

Many of the odds-beating schools made use of data to inform improvement efforts, including instruction. For example, at Ruby MS, the superintendent reported, "The culture here is that we don't rest on our laurels, but we keep looking at the data and the kids and wondering, 'How can we help them? How can we do better?'" Likewise, at Sage City MS, teachers said, "It's all data driven"; analyzing data "is a very big part" of "what we do here."

In addition to using data to inform instruction, educators in the odds-beating schools used data for long-term decision making. These schools not only had formal data systems, but they also had routines in place for teachers, administrators, and others to use data to drive goal setting and professional development priorities related to these goals. For example, educators at Yellow Valley ES use student data to align their goals to district goals. The goals of both district and school are specific, measurable, and heavily reliant upon student performance, which is reviewed monthly by the building planning team and teachers.

The use of data contributes to developing the vision, mission, and goals at Eagle Bluff ES, as well as providing indicators for evaluating progress. As a district leader explained,

> [We] do a gap analysis and say, "OK, in order to get to where we want to be five years from now, what are the things we're going to need to do; what are some

goals we're going to have to set for ourselves?" Understanding that—we also need to set measurable evaluation systems to mark our progress and map out our course, so to speak, and to make some mid-course corrections along the way.

These goals then drive the development of the building-, classroom-, and student-level goals. Each spring, the principal and school leadership team revisit the building-level goals to determine whether they have been met and to set goals for the coming school year.

The superintendent at Roaring Gap MS described a similar annual process of "very careful diagnostics" conducted with a range of stakeholders, explaining how this process identifies areas of student learning "we consider to be the most problematic, and they become our district priorities." From those priorities, the principal reported the development of annual building goals aligned with district priorities as well as identification of an additional building-level priority. As noted earlier, the superintendent credited this process of goal alignment with helping to promote coherence across the district, with each school contributing to the overall district goals.

Additionally, the superintendent noted the use of data for decision making at multiple levels: "When you really look at data and you can make informative decisions about a district program, or more importantly at the teacher level,

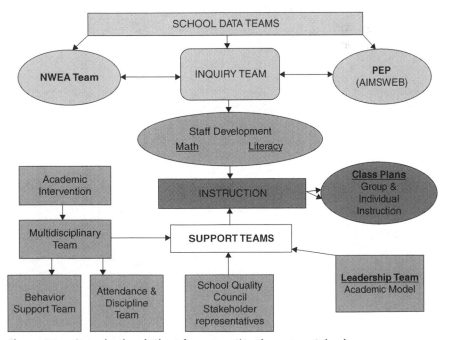

Figure 4.1. Organizational Chart from Bay City Elementary School

that's when you can really get into data-driven instruction." Another administrator stated, "We have a lot of data on every single student and we look at that by grade level, by school level, by district, and then we take those data to have conversations with administrators, with teachers, and with parents."

At Bay City ES, school and district leaders said they use data to identify professional development priorities. The superintendent reported that data analysis by principals and instructional coaches contributes to differentiation of professional development for different schools and grade levels and expressed a commitment to meet each school's needs. As shown in Figure 4.1, the school's data teams also play a key role in informing both professional development and instruction. In this way, data was a driver for two related priorities: Instruction and teachers' learning and professional development.

A CASE IN POINT—LARIBEE MIDDLE SCHOOL

All of our curriculum is electronic and in digital form. And teachers have their own individual maps based on district curriculum, and they can constantly be refining curriculum on their own individual maps with the understanding that when they come together as a department or a grade level, they're discussing a unit of study and different materials and different assessments. And they would bring that forward and they would collaborate and we would be having curriculum meetings to discuss those possibilities and those changes.

—district leader

The collaborative climate at Laribee Middle School supports the alignment of curriculum and instructional practices both within the school and across the district. This alignment can be attributed to the continual efforts of teachers, coaches, and administrators to reexamine curriculum and instructional practices, with an emphasis on innovation. These efforts are supported by professional development.

An ongoing effort to improve curriculum alignment throughout the district was mentioned repeatedly as an example of how leadership works in this district. An administrator said a key goal of this effort was to ease students' transitions between grade levels and schools. Led by the superintendent, a team that includes instructional specialists, department leaders, and resource teachers developed a detailed K-12 curriculum map that is made publicly available through an interactive tool on the district website.

Several teachers noted that teachers have some discretion over how to use the district curriculum map in aligning their instruction. From the central office to the school, staff members consistently described the curriculum as tightly aligned to the Common Core standards through the use of the district curriculum map. Teachers and leaders both said that they had begun working with district instructional coaches on making shifts to implement the Common Core standards prior to their adoption in the state, and the state curriculum modules were added to the instructional resources teachers could use in designing their lessons.

The teachers also have some discretion in terms of how much of their curriculum has been adopted specifically from the state curriculum modules. In many ways, this flexibility is derived from the fact that their curriculum had already been aligned with many of the aspects of the Common Core standards. This flexibility was supported by professional development and a "culture of risk taking" outlined by several district leaders and principals. All encouraged teachers to try new pedagogical techniques and share what works with their colleagues.

The district mathematics instructional coach described working with a committee of teachers to refine the curriculum, including tailoring units to meet student needs. This work included reorganizing topics to address teachers' observations that the unit on fractions was too long and grueling for fifth graders. The coach explained that the goal was to develop a firmer foundation of basic concepts through regular reinforcement before students tackle the more advanced topics closer to the time of the state assessments. Teachers reported being happier with the sequencing, and the coach reported that students are performing better on state assessments.

Both the English language arts (ELA) instructional coach and teachers also engaged in such curricular revision. They not only incorporated more nonfiction literature into the curriculum but also increased the focus on the core skills needed to do well on the state assessments. One of the department chairs noted that the grade-level teaming structure facilitates coordination with social studies to increase students' interaction with reading and writing.

A writing center provides resources to both students and teachers. An example of a core skill repeatedly mentioned by teachers was student use of text-based details to support their points.

Consistent with practices at the district level, teachers and school leaders described a collaborative decision-making structure regarding curriculum development. Teachers were encouraged to seek out new ideas with an eye for improvement of curriculum and instruction (Case in Point from Wilcox et al., 2015).

SUMMARY

At the odds-beating schools, existing processes for creating coherence and alignment supported innovation implementation and were instrumental in the progressive development of relational coherence and cross-organizational alignments. Using existing structures and mechanisms, educators were able to work slowly and intentionally over time to shift curriculum and classroom practice in line with the new mandates. District leaders also seized opportunities to tailor the CCSS, APPR, and DDI for the local context, inviting multiple voices to join the process, which resulted in genuine ownership of the three innovations.

Collective decision making and ownership helped maintain good will on the part of teachers and administrators who had to cohere around new routines and practices. In the odds-beating schools, this alignment and coherence provided scaffolding for district office and school leaders to "help it happen"—discussed in more detail in Chapter 8 (Greenhalgh, Robert, MacFarlane, Bate, & Kyriakidou, 2004).

Shared professional development furthered not only alignment of curriculum and instructional practices but also understanding of the essential work of the school and the district as a whole. These shared understandings were not evident in the typical performers. With clear expectations regarding curriculum and instruction, teachers in the odds beaters maintained significant professional discretion to adapt the standards to student needs and to take risks in doing so. Teachers in the typical performers experienced a more controlled, top-down approach.

Additionally, alignment mechanisms such as annual goal-setting meetings or monthly data meetings provided opportunities for the social processes that produce relational coherence, starting with collective sense making (Coburn, 2005). These activities provided structured opportunities for teachers and building leaders to engage in sense making within an environment of shared understanding of the goals and expectations for such meetings.

The strategic and regular use of multiple data sources by teachers and leaders in the odds-beating schools contributed to the ongoing examination of instructional practices, curriculum, and decision making. Such a data-driven strategy for making in-course corrections on the way to achieving long-term goals is a mechanism for organizational alignments, relational coherence, and continuous learning and improvement (Wilcox, Angelis, Lawson, 2015).

All in all, alignment and coherence allowed innovation & implementation to proceed in the odds-beating schools in a continuous rather than disruptive manner. This approach allowed them to maintain achievement levels while building on previous successes and facilitating learning and improvement over time. Leaders at the odds beaters understood their respective local contexts, had a clear vision, and adapted innovation requirements to meet that vision by integrating policy innovations with their own context-specific initiatives in order to create an integrated, aligned, and coherent approach to improvement.

REFERENCES

Bryk, A.S., Gomez, L.M., Grunow, A., & LeMahieu, P.G. (2015). *Learning to improve: How America's schools can get better at getting better.* Cambridge, MA: Harvard Education Press.

Christensen, C.M., Baumann, H., Ruggles, R., & Sadtler, T.M. (2006). Disruptive innovation for social change. *Harvard Business Review*, 84(12), 94.

Christensen, C.M., Horn, M.B., & Johnson, C.W. (2011). *Disrupting class: How disruptive innovation will change the way the world learns.* New York: McGraw Hill.

Coburn, C.E. (2005). Shaping teacher sensemaking: School leaders and the enactment of reading policy. *Educational Policy*, 19(3), 476–509.

Coburn, C.E., & Russell, J.L. (2008). District policy and teachers' social networks. *Educational Evaluation and Policy Analysis*, 30(3), 203–235. doi: 10.3102/0162373708321829

Daly, A.J., & Finnigan, K.S. (2016). The challenge of school and district improvement: Promising directions in district reform. In A.J. Daly & K.S. Finnigan (Eds.), *Thinking and acting systemically: Improving school districts under pressure* (pp. 229–241). Washington, DC: American Educational Research Association.

DuFour, R., & Fullan, M. (2013). *Cultures built to last: Systemic PLCs at work.* Bloomington, IN: Solution Tree Press.

Durand, F.T., Lawson, H.A., Wilcox, K.C., & Schiller, K.S. (2016). The role of district office leaders in the adoption and implementation of the Common Core State Standards in elementary schools. *Educational Administration Quarterly.* doi: 0013161X15615391

Fullan, M. (2006). *Turnaround leadership.* San Francisco: Jossey-Bass, Wiley Imprint.

Fullan, M., & Quinn, J. (2016) *Coherence: The right drivers in action for schools, districts and systems.* Thousand Oaks, CA: Corwin.

Greenhalgh, S., Robert, G., MacFarlane, F., Bate, P., & Kyriakidou, O. (2004). Diffusion of innovations in service organizations: Systematic review and recommendations. *The Milbank Quarterly*, 82(4), 581–629. doi:10.1111/j.0887-378x.2004.00325.x

Grossman, P., Hammerness, K.M., McDonald, M., & Ronfeldt, M. (2008). Constructing coherence: *Structural* predictors of perceptions of coherence in NYC teacher education programs. *Journal of Teacher Education*, 59(4), 273–287. doi:10.1177/0022487108322127

Hall, G.E. & Hord, S.M. (2006). *Implementing change: Patterns, principles, and potholes.* Boston: Allyn & Bacon.

Heifetz, R.A., Grashow, A., & Linsky, M. (2009). *The practice of adaptive leadership: Tools and tactics for changing your organization and the world.* Cambridge, MA: Harvard Business Press.

Honig, M.I., & Hatch, T.C. (2004). Crafting coherence: How schools strategically manage multiple, external demands. *Educational Researcher*, 33(8), 16–30. doi:10.3102/0013189x033008016

Johnson, S.S., Marietta, G., Higgins, M., Mapp, K., & Grossman, A. (2015). *Achieving coherence in district improvement: Managing the relationship between central office and schools.* Cambridge, MA: Harvard Education Press.

Knapp, M.S., Honig, M.I., Plecki, M.L., Portin, B.S., & Copland, M.A. (2014). *Learning-focused leadership in action: Improving instruction in schools and districts.* New York: Routledge.

Lawson, H.A., Durand, F.T., Wilcox, K.C., Gregory, K.M., Schiller, K.S., & Zuckerman, S.J. (2017). The role of district and school leaders' trust and communications in the simultaneous implementation of innovative policies. *Journal of School Leadership*, 27(1).

Senge, P., Cambron-McCabe, N., Lucas, T., Smith, B., Dutton, J., & Kleiner, A. (2012). *Schools that learn* (2nd Edition). New York: Crown Business.

Simmons, J. (2006). *Breaking through: Transforming urban school districts.* New York: Teachers College Press.

Wilcox, K.C., Angelis, J.I., & Lawson, H. (2015, October). *Developing capacities for evidence-guided continuous improvement: A university/P-12 network project.* Paper presented at the National Center on Scaling Up Effective Schools Annual Conference. Nashville, TN. Vanderbilt Peabody College.

Wilcox, K.C., Durand, F.T., Gregory, K., Schiller, K.S., Lawson, H., Zuckerman, S., Felicia, N., & Angelis, J.I. (2015). *Odds-beating middle schools cross-case report.* Prepared for the New York State Education Department as part of the School Improvement Study. Albany, NY: State University of New York.

Chapter Five

Readiness for Innovation

Francesca T. Durand and Hal A. Lawson

A growing body of research on innovation implementation highlights the important, if obvious, finding that preparing for change requires organizational readiness and capacity (McDonald, Klein, & Riordan, 2009; Weiner, 2009; Wilcox & Angelis, 2009). This is particularly true when external demands for change are initiated simultaneously and under tight timelines (Bryk, Gomez, Grunow, & LeMahieu, 2015; Hargreaves & Shirley, 2009; Knapp, Copland, Honig, Plecki, & Portin, 2014).

As discussed in the introduction of this book, disruptive innovations are designed to achieve a particular outcome by fundamentally altering an organization's processes and practices (Christensen, Horn, & Johnson, 2011). The Common Core State Standards (CCSS), annual professional performance reviews (APPR) based, in part, on student performance on CCSS assessments, and data-driven instruction (DDI), framed here as examples of such disruptive innovations, were designed to effect curricular and instructional changes in beneficial ways for both students and the adults who work with them in school.

Like many schools across the United States, the odds-beating schools in this study face the challenges of poverty, student transience, declining resources, and achievement gaps. Nevertheless, the educators within these schools strive to provide equal access to quality education for all students and to prepare all students to meet college- and career-readiness standards (Hatch, 2009; Holme & Rangel, 2012; Honig & Copland, 2014).

The challenges raise questions about how leaders are able to establish the conditions that make successful change possible (Greenhalgh, Robert, MacFarlane, Bate, & Kyriakidou, 2004; Malen et al., 2015). As discussed in earlier chapters, the underlying foundation of trust (Chapter 2), built and sustained by reciprocal communication (Chapter 3), and a clear and aligned vision, mission, and goals (Chapter 4), helped establish the conditions that made it possible for educators in the odds-beating schools to effectively meet the challenges of disruptive policy innovations, and to do so in ways that had desired, beneficial effects on teaching and learning.

Since performance generally declines as any workforce undertakes new routines, practices, and/or roles (Christensen et al., 2011; Kane, Owens, Marinell, Thal, & Staiger, 2016) one important question to ask is: Why and how were the odds-beating schools in this study able to implement the disruptive innovations without significant performance declines?

Clearly, the quality of leadership in both district and school is one factor that contributes to the ability to support rapid innovation. In particular, proactive leaders (Heifetz, Grashow, & Linsky, 2009; Weiner, 2009) are able to anticipate and prepare for change through resource allocation and leadership strategies of communication and trust building (Durand, Lawson, Wilcox, & Schiller, 2016).

A second factor is the readiness of the workforce to undertake the changes, supported by the resources needed—time, materials, adequate learning opportunities—to develop new competencies. And a third is the extent of professional discretion or "defined autonomy" (Waters & Marzano, 2009; Lawson et al., 2015) felt by the workforce.

This chapter describes how these three factors were demonstrated in the odds-beating schools, with contrasting examples drawn from the typical performers. The chapter closes with a representative case in point from one elementary school.

READINESS FOR CHANGE IN ODDS-BEATING SCHOOLS

Two primary questions related to organizational readiness for change framed this study of differences between odds-beating and typically performing schools. First, what organizational factors led to the readiness to adapt to the implementation of innovation in odds-beating schools? Second, how do these factors for readiness differ from what was seen in schools with typical performance?

Overall, readiness for change was critical in facilitating the adoption and implementation of the Common Core State Standards (CCSS). In particular, the following factors set the stage for an easier transition to the standards in the odds-beating elementary and middle schools:

- Proactive leadership;
- Strategic use of existing resources, including personnel, time, and funding, to facilitate change and foster trust and collaboration; and

- An organizational focus on developing defined autonomy and professional discretion.

The following sections describe each of these features and provide representative examples drawn from the elementary and middle schools studied.

Proactive Leadership

Proactive leaders continuously examine the internal and external environment for their organization and use what they learn to make decisions about the organization's long- and short-term goals, resource allocations, and internal workforce capacity (Weiner, 2009). They anticipate changes, develop organizational capacity and readiness, and help their organizations adapt and absorb innovations into current structures, programs, and policies (Durand et al., 2016).

Proactive leadership can partly account for the capacity of organizations to adopt innovations and to learn how to learn, thus further building capacity to continually be prepared for inevitable change (Hatch, 2009; Malen et al., 2015; Weiner, 2009). Educators across the odds-beating elementary and middle schools reported these leadership orientations and actions, and the leaders themselves identified them as critical to their schools' success in implementing the Common Core standards.

Leaders of all twelve odds-beating elementary and middle schools demonstrated proactive leadership when they implemented components of the standards prior to the state mandate. At the same time, they supported teachers as they worked to meet implementation challenges in their respective classrooms. At the district level, they developed and maintained a culture of trust that connected district office with the schools. Specifically, they relied on a potent combination of reciprocal trust and timely communications to facilitate structural alignments between the district office and the schools (Lawson et al., 2017).

At the school level, educators also reported anticipating the implementation of the standards and that principals and coaches worked as instructional leaders to guide teachers toward inevitable changes. One strategy was to employ Common Core-aligned curriculum prior to the state-mandated implementation date. In contrast, typically performing schools were generally reactive to the policy changes; teachers in the typical performers reported hurried implementation timelines to meet the state mandates and complained of lack of adequate preparation.

In order to implement Common Core-aligned curriculum in advance of the mandated timeline, leaders of odds-beating schools and districts had established cross-role curriculum teams a year or two in advance. For example, in

Ruby MS, the process began two years prior to the requirement. The super-intendent described the process as adaptation of existing curriculum, rather than adoption, saying,

> We've always looked at the standards. We've always adopted the standards of whatever has been expected, but we've always had the teachers write their own curriculum. And so whatever the rigor is that's expected is what we've used, and we've taken whatever we've needed to put into [that].

Teachers at Ruby work collaboratively to align the curriculum across grade levels and have historically been considered the curriculum experts best positioned to adapt the curriculum to meet state standards. However, as described by the principal, the initial reaction to the Common Core standards was hardly one of enthusiasm:

> In the middle school there was pandemonium and panic initially. . . . It was awful. But we had to be the peacekeepers. We had to keep saying, "You can do this. This isn't any different than what you normally do. . . . So just keep doing what you're doing."

Other examples of early, cross-role team planning come from Eagle Bluff and Yellow Valley elementary schools. In Eagle Bluff, the superintendent set up district-wide Common Core alignment curriculum teams a year before being directed to do so by the state. In Yellow Valley, district and school leaders were instrumental in instituting a new Common Core-aligned literacy curriculum a year prior to the state mandate.

As described in Chapter 3, teachers from Julesberg MS were sent by the district to learn more about the state's implementation plans a year in advance. These teams were then expected to share their learning with colleagues. Decisions about what to use to meet the state requirements for the CCSS and new APPR were made based on the recommendations of a committee of district and school leaders, teachers, and parents.

Today, district leaders in Julesberg rely on a collaborative style to make decisions about implementing the standards and related instructional shifts. The superintendent described this as making people "anxious to contribute" to the success of the school and district.

And in the district of Spring Creek ES, the superintendent explained that with a change as "huge" as the CCSS, it was important to work on implementing the changes early in order that teams of instructional leaders and teachers could take their time with implementation and get stakeholder feedback. Students in the odds-beating schools, then, had had more experience than students in typical performers with the new curriculum and instructional approaches when they took the first Common Core assessments, which were administered toward the end of the first year of the mandated implementation.

In contrast, not one superintendent representing a typically performing school reported any actions in anticipation of the implementation of the CCSS and performance evaluations based, in part, on student performance on CCSS assessments. No district official had put in place plans for teaching to the new standards before the mandated start date. They reported meeting the state's requirements during the year they were established, which sometimes led to stress on budgets as well as staff.

For example, the superintendent of Locus Glen MS described budget cuts that had forced staff reductions, further adding to workloads, as well as diverting funds to materials seen as necessary rather than to professional development:

> Last year, we spent thousands and thousands of dollars on the central text, which is all part of the ELA [state curriculum] modules, and you couldn't do the modules without it. So we bought everyone the central text because we had to. It's been really taking our PD money and then spending it on the Common Core—on the ELA and math side of it.

Overall, rather than being proactive, leaders of the typically performing schools were reactive to the new policy mandates.

Resource Allocations to Support Workforce Readiness

Adapting to new external demands such as the CCSS, new APPR, and data-driven instruction (DDI) requires considerable organizational readiness for change. Organizational readiness can be determined by looking at a variety of supportive features of schools and districts, such as deploying resources in new and different ways to meet new demands (Lawson et al., 2015; Johnson, Marietta, Higgins, Mapp, & Grossman, 2015; Malen et al., 2015).

In the odds-beating schools in this study, organizational readiness was facilitated in large part by provision of various forms of support to prepare teachers and staff for implementation of the innovations. In addition to a supportive trusting climate with strong communication patterns (see Chapters 2 and 3), these supports included:

- Maintaining collaborative structures such as teams and cross-role committees,
- Restructuring time and other resources to meet new needs,
- Reallocating budget lines and developing new resources, for example, through grant funding,

- Attending to emotional and interpersonal needs associated with change, and
- Providing professional development opportunities.

Using district resources in new, different or creative ways was reported by leaders of all twelve odds-beating schools. Resource reallocation was crucial in all the odds beaters because a decline in funding and other resources was universally reported. Leaders relied on a myriad of solutions to meet new needs and provide teachers with the resources necessary to learn to do their jobs differently.

An Urban Middle School Provides an Example

A robust and well-articulated example comes from Sage City MS. Leaders of this urban district spoke of striving to maintain a balanced approach between making sure to meet state regulations and providing the supports needed by school staff to make the necessary changes to curriculum and instruction. Leaders across school and district, including teachers, worked together to develop priorities and goals and decide how to meet challenges.

For example, district leaders described working collaboratively with school staff. The superintendent described the philosophy this way:

> A leader may be a conductor of sorts—a conductor of the orchestra—but you need everyone playing well at a high level and in tune and harmony. That's really how I see the role of leader in this modern era—as a conductor of an orchestra—but the orchestra is not made up of factory line workers but of skilled musicians.

Another important aspect of supporting a workforce to make disruptive changes—attending to the emotional and interpersonal needs of those required to learn fundamentally different modes of working and working together (Day & Lee, 2011; Fullan, 2011)—was described by an assistant superintendent. Referring, in particular, to teachers of special education, whose students often underperform on state assessments and whose assessment scores would now influence the teachers' performance reviews, he said,

> [The district] did a good job here. The teachers are . . . understanding of what the goal of Common Core is. Certainly I see special ed teachers being able to take the Common Core, and I can line you up in front of teachers who would tell you they think it's better for special ed kids because of the way it presents information. I think we did a great job with it.

The superintendent also described the processes of aligning expenditures to meet goals. This included strategically using resources to implement DDI:

We're trying to be creative by doing things like leveraging some outside streams of revenue. So that's one way and then looking at internal streams of revenue in different ways. I mean for instance, could we use some of the computer mediated instruction tools that are available now? . . . Part of the reason for the digital media isn't just because it's fun or colorful but because it can also track student data and present it back to the teacher. That can be a meaningful way to use data.

The example set by district leaders to coherently and systematically use time and resources differently was also seen at the school. The principal reported using team time to allow teachers to collaborate on curricular and instructional planning, discuss student data, and plan for other student needs. She defined change as hard and said, "I think APPR and Common Core have brought a lot of changes that have been difficult for a lot of people." But she also portrayed a school culture in which leaders and teachers work together to create a "positive place," with time and materials to do the needed work and the understanding that the work takes time and support.

Teachers also described a collaborative atmosphere with time for professional development, collaborative curricular development, and the freedom to ask for more resources if they need them. As discussed in Chapter 3, a teacher described goal setting as "top down and bottom up," with grade-level teachers setting goals together.

District leaders in Sage City made it a point to solicit feedback from school staff and then make adjustments where possible. This attention to the feelings and perceptions of school-level educators was a mark of leadership to set the stage for change in Sage City and all other odds-beating schools.

Reallocating Resources and/or Securing New Funds

Other schools whose leaders carefully examined funding streams and expenditures to reallocate resources to meet changing goals include Yellow Valley ES, where the superintendent reported a decline in resources and cuts in some programs. She also described using data to help reinstate programs and make decisions to cut less-effective programs. The district also used data to bring in grants and other external funds to hire instructional coaches and prioritize literacy at the elementary level through new curricular programs.

In Eagle Bluff ES, the superintendent described a collaborative process of resource allocation to make sure teachers have instructional and curricular materials, teachers' aides, and other resources needed to be able to teach to the new standards.

In contrast, no district leaders serving a typical performer described a reallocation of resources to support the new policies. In fact, they generally spoke only of declines in resources and the associated challenges to their work. For example, although two district leaders reported having access to external specialists for professional development purposes, they reported that they were using them less than before, due to budget cuts or time constraints.

In Tarelton MS, for example, the superintendent portrayed the implementation of the Common Core standards as "setting them back." He described having to make decisions to cut programs that had supported student after-school learning in order to meet budget needs for classroom materials and staff. He also said that prior to the implementation of the standards and new APPR process the small rural district had had the ability to collectively make decisions. Now, however, he felt he had to make the difficult decisions; despite seeking feedback from school staff, he saw the budget as leaving him no choices.

Others in Tarelton agreed. Educators at both school and district levels spoke repeatedly of not having the resources necessary to meet all the needs of students in special education, students with disabilities, and students living in poverty. Shifting resources to meet these students' needs would take resources away from previous commitments to professional development and curricular development. As a result, teachers were spending less time collaborating than they had before implementing the Common Core standards.

Collaborating to Support Change

At Eagle Bluff ES, despite resource challenges and increasing demands, administrators preserved structures for groups of teachers to work on curriculum collaboratively. They explained that they kept processes for aligning goals from the district to the classroom in place, as these were seen as contributing to educators' abilities to adapt to changes. So, too, in Spring Creek ES, where administrators said that they worked collaboratively with educators in the schools to make tough decisions to meet district goals, focusing on instruction, professional development around the Common Core standards, and software.

In Laribee MS, district leaders reconfigured team times to allow for collaborative work on developing Common Core-aligned instruction, provided funding and time for professional development to meet building-level needs, and distributed goal setting and other leadership activities throughout the district. For example, an assistant superintendent described multiple district-wide groups and committees consisting of teacher leaders, other school leaders, and parent councils that play various roles in decision making. This process helps to align school and district mission and to meet goals (Honig & Hatch, 2004).

The principal of Laribee characterized the district as supportive of the school and the school as supportive of the district goals, saying,

We follow the directives set by the district. And we have a building action plan that aligns with the district action plan. . . . We look at best practices . . . as a district, we are looking specifically at project-based learning and at differentiated instruction. I was part of the professional development group last year that brought a local professional developer to the district [to help with that work].

She further described the school as the implementer of the district's action plan, which was collaboratively developed by teachers and staff members in the schools. Teachers and school staff concurred that they had support from the district for their implementation of the Common Core standards through professional development, shifting of finances to get needed resources, and the collaborative nature of the district in both deciding on and meeting goals. An instructional coach at the middle school described their ability to ask for resources:

We're also lucky we do get . . . most resources. If we want something we can request it. I mean it's not that the sky's the limit . . . it's a school, [but] we do have a lot. . . . We are also people rich. We have terrific special education staffs, we have the reading teachers, the librarian. I think it really is that team—it goes back to that team, family; we are all in this together.

Typically performing schools were less likely to have established or maintained structures designed to support educators to work together to change practice and meet new requirements.

Professional Discretion and Defined Autonomy

Another feature of organizational readiness for change in odds-beating elementary and middle schools was a climate of professional discretion and defined autonomy for both building leaders and teachers. Overall, these schools and districts had been able to find the balance between too tight and too loose control over instructional practice (Fullan, 2006).

District leaders set the tone for this practice by setting clear goals for learning and instruction while giving school leaders responsibility for meeting those goals, what Waters and Marzano (2009) termed "defined autonomy." This model of leadership allowed for principals and teacher leaders to be instructional leaders in the way that worked best for their particular student populations.

Also discussed in Chapter 2, teachers in the odds-beating schools enjoyed the right amount of professional discretion. Survey and interview results show that teachers in eleven of the twelve odds-beating schools (five elementary schools and six middle schools) felt safe to implement the Common Core standards using their professional judgment and that they received district and school leaders' messages of support to do so. In interviews, they described being treated as professionals trusted to make instructional decisions about what worked best in providing standards-aligned instruction to all children in their particular classrooms. As one Spring Creek ES teacher put it,

> I have a cousin who teaches in a neighboring district, and they were not happy with the [state curriculum] modules, but they have been told they have to continue [using them]. I have been teaching the same material, but [our] superintendent has given us the freedom to make adjustments and use our professional judgment [if something] isn't working.

As a Spring Creek administrator explained, teachers trust leaders "with a lot of the big decisions," and leaders trust teachers "to make the best decisions for their kids."

A district leader of Starling Springs ES explained the importance of such professional autonomy:

> I acknowledge and think very deeply about personal agency and efficacy. . . . I believe the agents of change are [that] something internal has changed or clicked or connected—either you have experienced some small level of success and you are seeing it for yourself, like, "Oh, I taught this, this way; this happened. OK let me try something else"—or a credible leader or colleague has tried something, and that has been successful . . .—vicarious experiences—that leads me to do something different.
>
> And so all of that to me is related to our mission of empowerment because basically we are not saying, "Do what we say because we have this authority and we're leaders," but, "Try this, empower yourselves as educators and have that lead you to different practices, a different belief system, different ways of engaging students." And we personally . . . believe as a team that that is the path towards change: Individuals making individual small decisions every day to do things differently to engage students—not because of the new mandate or memo or regulation.

District and school administrators at Starling Springs indicated that they understood the "too tight, too loose dilemma" (Fullan, 2006) and said that they adhered to the motto of staying "tight on outcomes and loose on process," allowing teachers to teach to the standards in a relatively unscripted manner. A district administrator explained that that approach had started before the mandated implementation date:

> We were developing curriculum and units well before the modules were put out, and frankly our stuff is better. We've given people that flexibility. I'm going to hold them [teachers] accountable for those key metrics, and as long as they

continue the shift, I don't care if they use a module, a lesson plan found on line or video-chatted somebody in. I don't care to be honest with you. . . . We've been very loose about what they use.

Teachers at Starling Springs confirmed that are trusted to make instructional decisions based on their own judgment within the context of shared expectations.

A pattern of providing support for teachers' instructional practice and communicating that there was flexibility in the curricular paths of implementing the Common Core standards was evident in all the odds-beating middle schools.

For example, in Julesberg MS, leaders sought teachers' input regarding the use of Common Core-aligned curriculum modules provided by the state. In 2013, they had required that ELA teachers use one curriculum module with 100% fidelity; however, after voicing strong dissatisfaction with this decision, teachers were given the option of adapting the modules as they saw fit. Likewise, math teachers were not mandated to use the modules. Instead, they collaborated within grade levels to create their own instructional materials.

In Roaring Gap MS, although district administrators expressed an expectation that teachers follow the curriculum maps and calendars, the need for flexibility in teaching the curriculum was also respected and accepted. One district leader stated,

I think that they [the teachers] do need flexibility and they do need to explore their own path of instruction. So if one teacher is more apt to incorporate more fish bowl as a strategy or more technology as a strategy, I want them to have that flexibility, but standards are consistent, and the core text is consistent, and we have developed a calendared curriculum so that we know when different standards are going to be taught and assessed.

Special education teachers at Roaring Gap also reported flexibility in working with their students, teaching things in multiple ways, depending on the learner. The emphasis on flexible implementation related to the emphasis on differentiated instruction to meet individual needs was identified by the superintendent and other district leaders.

Finally, the leaders of odds-beating schools in this study were flexible about the CCSS implementation timetables. In other words, they advocated for and allowed teachers to take the time to try out and adjust the pacing of the state curriculum modules to see what worked in their own classrooms. They introduced the modules to a few classrooms at a time and provided professional development and time for teams to work together on the implementation. They also regularly sought feedback from teachers and parents and used data to inform decisions about instruction and curriculum.`

The Eagle Bluff superintendent reported how the district proceeded with implementation:

> So we know that learning isn't static and that what we're asked to do and what we're preparing kids for isn't static. So what we need to do is have a system that will allow us to evolve. And this, the way that we have things working, allows us to evolve. What I said to the teachers was, "What do you need? How much time do you need? How do you want to go about this?"
>
> In other words, "Do you want release time, work after school? Do you want to focus it just on the summer because you've got kids and there's always this balance of how much time can people take out of their classroom and still feel like they're doing their work?" I don't dictate how that's to be done. I said, "The standards are here; let's take a look at these and see where are we in terms of what we need to be doing and where are the gaps." So they started looking at that and made the adjustments in the curriculum.

In contrast, the characteristics of odds-beating schools described above were either not evident or not prevalent at typically performing schools. For example, at the suburban Sun Hollow ES, school and district leaders spoke of using the state mandates to spark changes in curriculum and instruction that they said were not possible without external pressure. They spoke of leveraging the standards and the modules specifically to put into place what a teacher described as "an aligned and prioritized curriculum," something they had not been able to do prior to the implementation of the CCSS.

In Tarelton MS, the leadership team had not implemented a structured way to determine how the standards would be implemented district-wide; resulting in a too loose interpretation by teachers, who each reported a different plan across grade levels and classrooms.

A CASE IN POINT—STARLING SPRINGS ELEMENTARY SCHOOL

We incorporate new ideas into what we already do.

— teacher

"We were doing those standards before they were called the Common Core," said one administrator, or put more colorfully by a teacher: "It's not like we replaced candy with broccoli with candy; we replaced broccoli with cauliflower or carrots." In general, district and school administrators tried to incorporate the Common Core initiative into existing philosophies and processes rather than completely overhaul curriculum and instruction. The general feeling expressed by educators was the importance of "keeping their roots" and building on the success they had developed over time rather than throwing out the old to start the new.

A multi-faceted and proactive approach to managing the changes required by the state entailed strategic and planned actions. These actions included:

1. Ensuring that teachers learned the standards and providing the resources needed to achieve this goal.
2. A focus on the standards (rather than the assessments or evaluations based on those assessments), which created conditions that allowed teachers to feel supported to take their own initiative rather than feel "railroaded" into teaching to the standards.
3. A process through which teachers were able to access new tools and new ideas in order to gradually implement the standards and make the necessary instructional shifts, using such resources as the Singapore Math program.
4. Encouraging each teacher to choose one state ELA curriculum module to use initially, with support from an instructional coach.

The consensus among administrators and teachers was that teachers had fully embraced the standards and placed a high value on the concepts that guide them. Many teachers noted that the Common Core emphasis on thinking skills aligns well with what they have always done.

Additionally, many teachers noted that they had been given the supports needed to put the standards into place in their classroom. "I absolutely feel that they are an excellent set of standards, and I feel that I understand them very, very well. I feel that we have been given a lot of professional development around unpacking the standards and understand them and understand that they are just that—standards not a curriculum," explained a teacher.

The district philosophy of helping everyone to feel both prepared and unpressured extended to students. Educators described efforts to help students develop confidence and perspective as they focus on learning rather than testing. "We make it a very relaxed type atmosphere—not pressure, pressure, pressure," said one teacher, as her grade-level colleagues nodded in agreement.

Perhaps because district and school leaders have kept the focus on how the standards foster higher levels of student thinking and academic engagement, parents and community members were reported to have been accepting and sometimes enthusiastic about them. One teacher spoke to this, saying,

People are very involved in their student's education; trust is very high between parents and teachers here, and parents take the ownership to make sure that their child's getting the work done and . . . doing it well. And as a teacher, I feel like if you have that, it helps because my own personal view on it is, I don't care if a student of mine makes sense out of a concept from hearing it from me, or hearing it from a parent, or working with an afterschool counselor or teacher, as long as they've learned it.

District and school websites and other communications provided information on the standards early and often and report on particular curriculum elements that bring excitement to classrooms. When parents see how teachers blend the new initiatives into dynamic, student-centered lessons, they cannot help but feel positive about it, faculty members commented, noting that they have largely avoided the community tension that comes with overemphasis on student test scores or teacher evaluation processes (Case in Point taken from Wilcox et al., 2014).

SUMMARY

Together, the odds-beating schools and their district offices show how educators' abilities to respond to the new policy mandates were built on previous strategies and accomplishments. The historical-developmental patterns within these organizations helped to account for their readiness to make disruptive changes, in part because of the actions of proactive district office leaders, past and present.

Superintendents in particular set the foundation in several ways. First, they proactively approached the concepts of the anticipated Common Core standards as well as the new accountability measures for educators. Indeed, some district leaders had implemented prequels to the standards, performance evaluations, and DDI before the state mandates.

Further, district and school leaders used their local community contexts, student population needs, and district goals to influence innovation implementation. They ruled out a "one-size-fits-all strategy" and worked collaboratively with school leaders and teachers to facilitate implementation, aligning and cohering as they went.

Additionally, leaders strategically used existing resources, including personnel, time, and funding, to facilitate change and foster trust and collaboration. They also actively sought out new resources from a variety of sources, including grants, state funds, and partnerships with new organizations.

Finally, leaders encouraged and promoted the use of professional discretion and defined autonomy for principals, teachers and instructional staff as they implemented the standards. In all, district and school leaders in odds-beating schools use a combination of these actions, in a climate that encourages reciprocal communication and trust, to set the stage for innovation implementation.

REFERENCES

Bryk, A., Gomez, L., Grunow, A., & LeMahieu, P. (2015). *Learning to improve: How America's schools can get better at getting better*. Cambridge, MA: Harvard Education Press.

Christensen, C.M., Horn, M.B., & Johnson, C.W. (2011). *Disrupting class: How disruptive innovation will change the way the world learns*. New York: McGraw Hill.

Day, C. & Lee, J.C., Eds. (2011). *New understandings of teacher's work: Emotions and educational change*. The Netherlands: Springer.

Durand, F.T., Lawson, H.A., Wilcox, K.C., & Schiller, K.S. (2016). The role of district office leadership in the adoption and implementation of the Common Core State Standards in elementary schools. *Educational Administration Quarterly*, 51(1), 45–74. doi:10.1177/0013161x15615391

Fullan, M. (2006). *Turnaround leadership*. San Francisco: Jossey-Bass, Wiley Imprint.

Fullan, M. (2011). *Change leader: Learning to do what matters most*. San Francisco: Jossey-Bass.

Greenhalgh, S., Robert, G., MacFarlane, F., Bate, P., & Kyriakidou, O. (2004). Diffusion of innovations in service organizations: Systematic review and recommendations. *The Milbank Quarterly*, 82(4), 581–629. doi:10.1111/j.0887-378x.2004.00325.x

Hargreaves, A. & Shirley, D. (2009). The persistence of presentism. *Teachers College Record*, iii(11), 2505–2534.

Hatch, T. C. (2009). *Managing to change: How schools can survive (and sometimes thrive) in turbulent times*. New York: Teachers College Press.

Heifetz, R., Grashow, A. & Linsky, M. (2009). *The practice of adaptive leadership: Tools and tactics for changing your organization and the world*. Boston, MA: Harvard Business Press.

Holme, J.J., & Rangel, V.S. (2012). Putting school reform in its place: Social geography, organizational social capital, and school performance. *American Educational Research Journal*, 49(2), 257–283. doi: 10.3102/0002831211423316.

Honig, M.I., & Copland, M.A. (2014). Conditions supportive of central office leadership for instructional improvement. In M.S. Knapp, M. Honig, M. Plecki, B. Portin, & M. Copland (Eds.). *Learning-focused leadership in action: Improving instruction in schools and districts* (pp. 102–120). New York: Routledge.

Honig, M.I., & Hatch, T.C. (2004). Crafting coherence: How schools strategically manage multiple, conflicting demands. *Educational Researcher*, 33(8), 16–30. doi:10.3102/0013189x033008016

Johnson, S.S., Marietta, G., Higgins, M., Mapp, K., & Grossman, A. (2015). *Achieving coherence in district improvement: Managing the relationship between central office and schools*. Cambridge, MA: Harvard Education Press.

Kane, T.J., Owens, A.M., Marinell, W.H., Thal, D.R., & Staiger, D.O. (2016). *Teaching higher: Educators' perspectives on Common Core implementation.* Cambridge, MA: Center for Education Policy Research, Harvard University.

Knapp, M.S., Copland, M.A., Honig, M.I., Plecki, M.L., & Portin, B.S. (2014). *Practicing and supporting learning-focused leadership in schools and districts.* New York: Routledge.

Lawson, H.A., Durand, F.T, Wilcox, K.C., Gregory, K., Schiller K.S. & Zuckerman, S (2017). The role of district and school leaders' trust and communications in the simultaneous implementation of policy innovations. *Journal of School Leadership,* 27(1).

Lawson, H.A, Wilcox, K.C., Gregory, K., Durand, F., Angelis, J.I, Schiller, K.S., & Zuckerman, S.J. (2015). *Comparing and contrasting odds-beating elementary and middle schools: Toward a theory of action.* A report for the New York State Education Department as part of the School Improvement Study. Albany, NY: State University of New York.

Malen, B., Rice, J., Matlach, L., Bowsher, A., Hoyer, K. & Hyde, L. (2015). Developing organizational capacity for implementing complex education reform initiatives: Insights from a multiyear study of a teacher incentive fund program. *Educational Administration Quarterly,* 51(1), 133–176. doi: 10.1177/0013161X14522482

McDonald, J., Klein, E., & Riordan, M. (2009). *Going to scale with new school designs: Reinventing high school.* New York: Teachers College Press.

Waters, J.T. & Marzano, R.J. (2007). The primacy of superintendent leadership. *School Administrator* 64(3), 10–16.

Weiner, B. J. (2009). A theory of organizational readiness for change. *Implementation Science,* 4(67). doi:10.1186/1748-5908-4- 67

Wilcox, K.C. & Angelis, J.I. (2011). *Best practices from high-performing high schools.* New York: Teachers College Press.

Wilcox, K.C., Durand, F.T., Schiller, K.S., Gregory, K. Zuckerman, S., Felicia, N., Angelis, J. I., & Lawson, H. (2014). *Odds-beating elementary school cross-case report.* Prepared for the New York State Education Department as part of the School Improvement Study. Albany, NY: State University of New York.

Chapter Six

Instructional Adaptation

Kristen Campbell Wilcox

As highlighted throughout this book, the Common Core State Standards and use of student performance results on Common Core assessments to inform teacher and principal evaluations were intended to provide better and more opportunities for all students to develop the knowledge and skills to be college or career ready. However, as has been the case in past reform efforts, implementation of educational innovations can be associated with performance declines for teachers and students alike and can result in a variety of unintended and unexpected consequences in classrooms.

Two unanticipated consequences of combining implementation of new standards and new assessments with high-stakes consequences for teachers are particularly important: One is the potential of narrowing instruction to what is assessable and assessed. The second is movement away from practices like inclusion and coteaching that can be particularly advantageous for English-language learners and students with disabilities as teachers fear students' relatively poor assessments will reflect badly on them (Honigsfeld & Dove, 2012; Wehmeyer, Field, Doren, Jones, & Mason, 2004; York-Barr, Ghere, & Sommerness, 2007; Ysseldyke, Nelson, Christenson, Johnson, Dennison, Triezenberg, & Hawes, 2004).

Intuitively it would seem that the push for more rigorous standards for all students and for teachers and principals to be at least partially accountable for results makes sense and would benefit everyone. However, implementing multiple innovations simultaneously and rapidly and with what some consider insufficient public and other stakeholder input as well as ones that could work at cross-purposes sets up the potential for performance declines and resistance. This is especially true in schools with highly challenged populations of students, insufficient resources to meet student needs, and poor organizational capacities (Darling-Hammond, 2010).

In light of these challenges, this chapter is guided by the following question: How do educators in the odds-beating schools adapt their instruction to new standards and assessments without performance declines and with relatively little resistance?

To respond to this question, it is necessary to identify how instructional adaptations relate to reducing the potential for performance declines during times of rapid change and how they work in both an anticipatory (i.e., learning and applying something different or new prior to required change) and a reactive way (i.e., learning and applying something different or new when performance declines have already occurred in response to some external change) (Jundt, Shoss, & Huang, 2014).

PERFORMANCE ADAPTATION IN CLASSROOMS

The concept of performance adaptation focuses our lens on phenomena that occur during the implementation of innovations such as the CCSS (e.g., Baard, Rench, & Kozlowski, 2014). Baard et al. (2014), in a review of the literature, define performance adaptation as: "the cognitive, affective, motivational, and behavioral modifications made in response to the demands of a new or changing environment or situational demands" (p. 50).

While the literature regarding instructional practices and how they relate to student achievement outcomes is immense, a few particular lines of inquiry provide important foregrounding for the discussion of what was found with regard to performance adaptation in the odds-beating schools. These include: the relationships of student performance and data-driven instruction (DDI) systems, differentiated instruction, self-regulated and higher-order thinking, nurturing and inclusive classroom climates, and collaborative school cultures.

In brief and with regard to DDI, what performance data are generated, how data are accessed, how they are discussed, and how they are used have all been found to be important features in schools with better-than-expected student performance outcomes (Angelis & Wilcox, 2011; Datnow & Hubbard, 2015; Honig & Venkateswaran, 2012; Knapp, Honig, Plecki, Portin, & Copland, 2014; Spillane, 2012).

In Datnow and Hubbard's study, for example, while teachers were found to be using benchmark assessment data, variations in the effectiveness of data use were identified and related to school- and district-wide agendas for data use, the nature of the assessments, and teacher beliefs about how data relate to their instructional choices.

A great deal of research has investigated instructional strategies that might explain achievement gaps in different schools. This research often highlights differentiation strategies (i.e., using more than one-way, teacher-led interactions, varying groupings, materials, and tasks) to better meet the needs of diverse learners. Such differentiation has been indicated as a factor related to better achievement among diverse students in study after study (e.g., Hiebert, 2006; Reis, McCoach, Little, Muller, & Kaniskan, 2011; Kiemer, Gröschner, Pehmer, & Seidel, 2015; National Reading Panel, 2000; Wilcox, Lawson, & Angelis, 2015).

For many teachers, the learning curve is steep as they grapple with changing practice. This is especially true when they are faced with multiple changes such as using DDI to inform their practice and aligning instruction to new curriculum and standards.

As mentioned briefly in Chapter 1 of this book, the key instructional changes required to align to the Common Core standards have been termed the "shifts," one of which is a stronger emphasis on students developing independence as learners. In fact, the word "independent" appears 26 times in a 43-page document detailing the "Research Supporting Key Elements of the Standards" (Council of Chief State School Offers & National Governors Association, 2010). Yet, how teachers might translate this "independence" into practice with diverse learners, some with needs for more scaffolding and some with not as much, requires clarification, modeling, and practice.

Accompanying this shift to a stronger emphasis on independence is an emphasis on higher-order thinking that includes the ability to analyze multiple texts to assert an argument or make a claim. Here, again, the research has suggested that these skills are inherently difficult and raise challenges for many students. This is particularly true for those with lower performance histories who may not have had to engage in much—or even any—such work prior to the implementation of the CCSS (Olson, Scarcella, & Matuchniak, 2015).

A final area of related research regards the role of engaging classroom climates within collaborative school cultures, discussed in Chapters 2 and 5, in particular. Allington (2010), among others, has asserted that supportive and caring teachers matter more than "proven" programs or approaches and in order for teachers to express their best teaching, they need both high-quality mentoring and collaborative school cultures.

Schools can be seen as one of the essential fibers of the fabric of a society as expressed in Chapter 1 of this book. Extending this metaphor and in alignment with social ecological theory, curriculum and instruction might be seen as essential threads in the fabric of schools. They can be seen as the interwoven fibers of this fabric, drawing attention to the interplay of both (1) individual teachers' and students' characteristics and (2) organizational capacities for adaptation.

Adapting Curriculum and Instruction in Odds-Beating Schools

Teachers in the odds-beating schools had managed to adapt their instruction to maintain both academic rigor and connection of the curriculum to their own students' lives while integrating the emphases of the CCSS. In some cases, this raised the bar considerably in terms of the level of performance expected of students as well as the kind of thinking in which they engaged. Likewise, teachers were required to learn new ways of engaging children with content, taking into account stronger emphasis on particular twenty-first-century skills and competencies discussed earlier.

These adaptations included: (1) adoption of an evidence-guided system to facilitate the regular use of a variety of data to inform instructional adaptations, (2) widespread use of differentiation strategies in a problem-specific, user-centered approach focused on variations in performance, (3) a focus on higher-order thinking and self-regulation skills, and (4) nurturing an engaging, inclusive, supportive classroom climate within a broader collaborative and inclusive school culture. Each of these was facilitated by either district- or school-wide professional development and mentoring. Figure 6.1 displays these four features contributing to CCSS implementation.

The next section describes each of these characteristics of odds-beating schools. The chapter concludes with a case in which these four themes come to life in an elementary school.

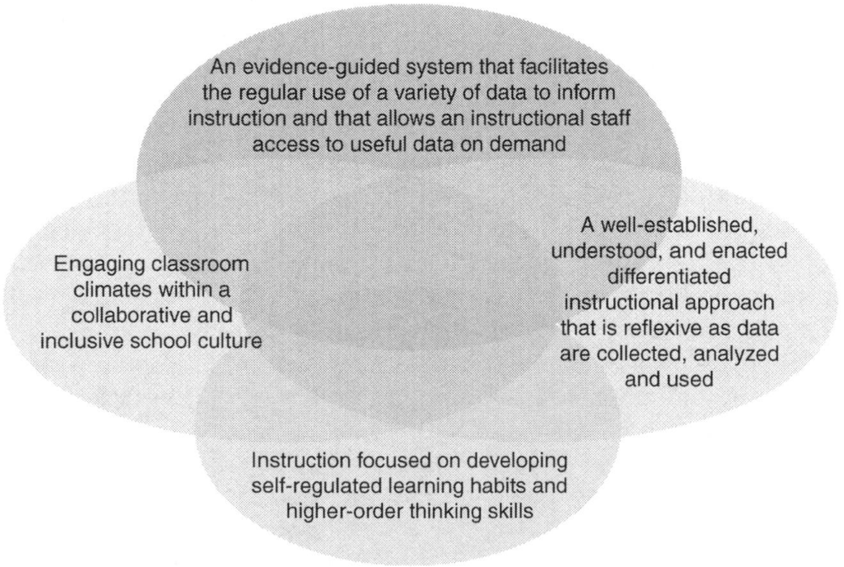

An evidence-guided system that facilitates the regular use of a variety of data to inform instruction and that allows an instructional staff access to useful data on demand

Engaging classroom climates within a collaborative and inclusive school culture

A well-established, understood, and enacted differentiated instructional approach that is reflexive as data are collected, analyzed and used

Instruction focused on developing self-regulated learning habits and higher-order thinking skills

Figure 6.1.   The Four Interrelated Features of Instruction in Odds-Beating Schools

Data-Driven Instruction

As highlighted in the literature cited in Chapter 1 of this book (e.g., Cohen & Moffitt, 2009), producing assessment data (on both student and teacher performance) without pathways for their interpretation and use is not likely to improve outcomes. Indeed, one of the distinctive characteristics of the odds-beating schools in this study relates to data and their use.

Focusing on the middle schools in the study, while two typically performing schools (Silver City and Locus Glen) showed some evidence of systems that placed data within reach of teachers on demand, neither they nor the third typical performer (Tarelton) demonstrated other attributes of DDI to the extent that their odds-beating counterparts did. For example, the odds beaters were characterized by a formalized and functional DDI system that makes the generation and use of a variety of data part of educators' routines to adapt instruction in real time. Such systems go beyond just making data available to educators.

An instructional survey administered to all teaching staff as part of this study bore out the contrast in data use. It revealed that educators in odds-beating schools (approximately 57%) reported that they were likely to participate with colleagues in looking at data at least once a week; fewer of their peers in typically performing schools (approximately 35%) reported a similar frequency of discussions centered on data.

Although this difference is marginally statistically significant ($p < 1$), when combined into an index with "participating in professional development" and "practicing new skills," the differences at the middle school level are statistically significant ($p < 0.05$). Fifty-three percent of teachers in odds-beating middle schools reported doing at least two of these activities a week: analyzing data, participating in professional development, or practicing new skills. In contrast, only 28% of teachers in typically performing schools reported doing at least two of these activities a week.

Furthermore, interview and focus group data from all schools suggest that beyond the frequency of dialogues about data, one of the characteristics of the DDI systems in the odds-beating schools relates to the content and quality of the data generated and used (Datnow & Hubbard, 2015). Another relates to how data are accessed and used (Honig & Venkateswaran, 2012; Knapp et al., 2014; Spillane, 2012).

With regard to content and quality of the data they were generating, the main difference between the two groups of schools involves whether and how educators developed and used assessments to check students' performance using Common Core assessment-like quizzes and tests.

While "teaching to the test" carries generally negative connotations, many educators interviewed in the odds-beating schools hold the view that "sprinkling" such assessments throughout the school day (in "exit tickets," for example) and throughout the school year (in periodic benchmarks, for example) provides students the needed practice. This practice is both in terms of procedures for taking the assessments and in terms of engaging with the content of the assessments themselves.

In odds-beating middle schools like Hutch Hill, Laribee, and Roaring Gap, teachers developed quizzes to look like items on the state assessments, and the responses to these quizzes were graded using the same rubrics as for the state assessments. A Hutch Hill eighth-grade teacher described what data these formative assessments were providing teachers and students:

> Most of our quizzes are aligned to look like the [state] tests will look. We try to make short answers similar to what they will do on the ELA assessment. We do so much looking at previous ones, asking, "Why was this [answer scored] a four, three, or two?" They [students] know all the trips and tips on how to do well on the assessment.

In Laribee MS, the rationale for using such assessments was clearly seen as being in the students' best interests. As a teacher explained,

> I would never want a student to think that he or she was not prepared. I mean it's a hefty little packet that gets dropped on your desk for each of the three days [of the state assessment], and so we try to talk through what that experience is going to be like. Ninety minutes is a long time to just look at one thing, so some of it is just talking through what that experience is going to look like without giving them six practice 90-minute experiences.

And in an example from Roaring Gap MS, the superintendent spoke to how teachers have been central in thinking through the CCSS content, poring over state assessment questions, and developing assessments that will yield the kinds of data they need to make instructional adaptations appropriate for their students:

> Teachers have developed assessments that mirror the state assessments. The state has put out questions to share, so just using that information and using what they put out before and using the [state curriculum] modules, and that kind of thing, as a guide. . . . I really think that's kind of why we're doing as well as we are.

An alternative approach to the aforementioned scenario of integrating Common Core assessment-like material in regular formative and benchmark assessments is to wait for state assessment results to be released to then modify instruction or curricular materials. It is here that the differences of typically performing schools with odds-beating schools become clear.

In the typically performing schools, teachers expressed frustration with not being able to plan for instruction as they waited for state assessment results to be released. "We are reactive to the test now; before, we used to be proactive," said a teacher from Locus Glen MS. And in Silver City MS, the principal conceded that while they have Common Core benchmarks they "are not very good."

An important note about the formative assessment data produced in the odds-beating schools also must be made here. This note relates to the extent of autonomy that teachers in these schools reported having in designing and implementing different types of formative assessments.

The following quote from a teacher at odds-beating Hutch Hill MS captures the essence of a pattern noted in the data from odds-beating schools in general. It speaks to the importance placed on keeping the content and shape of summative assessments consistent across classrooms, while leaving the content and shape of formative assessments up to the determination of the teacher. This provides a balance between the "too tight/too loose" dilemma discussed in the literature (e.g., Fullan, 2006; Hargreaves & Fullan, 2012) by maintaining teacher choice in how learning is assessed on a day-to-day basis (see also Fullan, Rincón-Gallardo, & Hargreaves, 2015).

> We look at curriculum, whether it's tight or loose—because we're in the PLCs, so we start at the end, what our summative assessments are. We all do the exact same summative assessments. Formatively you get there the way you want to get there, because we feel like, how do we determine best practices if we're all lock-step doing the same thing with everything? We don't have any juice then, so to speak, with each other, to say, "Hey, I took it here and I got a whole other piece of learning." When we lock-stepped, personally, it was stifling for improvement. —Hutch Hill MS teacher

This last statement touches on some very important implications about innovative school systems that defy typical performance trajectories for their diverse students. They are schools in which people are actively making sense of data and are doing so in personally relevant ways, yet within teams that provide opportunities for collective sense making. The fact that this combination of factors is in play in the odds-beating schools and, as the teacher cited earlier expressed, relates to their motivations for continuous improvement offers a host of implications (discussed in more detail in Chapter 8).

Next, however, a second finding related to data highlights the import of data access and use. Ready access to data that help track individual students' growth is an important quality of a data system in any school. Technologies can provide readily accessible data to help inform instruction. At odds-beating Laribee and Sage City middle schools, for example, students are encouraged to use smartphone apps such as Socrative Student, which they use to answer questions in response to teachers' assignments. Two teachers in Laribee recounted how they access and use these data for instruction:

> *T1:* You can log in under your name, but your name isn't displayed. They [students] all see the answers on the board, and then we can discuss what the answers are, but no one's name is associated with that answer.

> *T2:* And what's nice is you can send the results to yourself in an email. So in the leisure of those after-school hours you can look at those Excel spreadsheets, you can look at the students by name. So even though you can hide students' names when it's on display [in class], you can look at those names and assess your data and say, "Okay who really understands this, and does it surprise me that she didn't get that question right?" or "I'm noticing that all of these kids missed this," or "My second period really didn't understand this, but my third period did. What happened in second period that didn't happen in third period?" It's really a way to refine your instruction.

At Ruby MS, teachers described a data system that allows teachers access to both individual students' and whole cohorts' performances on demand. These data yield a holistic view of the effectiveness of the curriculum and their instruction across grade levels. As one teacher explained,

> We traditionally have good math scores. Sixth, seventh, and eighth [grade] math here are the highest in [the region]. If you track them through, two grade levels were weaker coming in—last year's and this year's sixth graders were struggling the most. We can see how a student improved individually and can track that as well as the general population.

Data Analysis and Use

One of the contrasts between the odds-beating and typically performing schools is nuanced. It relates to the degree to which educators are drilling down into their data to glean implications for their practice and how this is done collaboratively. Of the twelve odds-beating schools studied, more than half of them showed evidence of particularly progressive and effective processes for doing this. In the following example, a Laribee teacher explains the level of specificity ("nuts and bolts") their PLC gets into when discussing student performance data.

> We try to say the data that we want to work with is down to the nuts and bolts—the practical. So when I'm looking at data, what I'm looking at is, "Is there a particular standard that our students did well on compared to the . . . region around us?" So we can do some comparisons and we find the places [where]

we are succeeding, and we can chase it back to the unit. "These are great, this is wonderful, let's keep doing what we're doing here."

An important feature of this work is how it is catalyzed through teams using data to inform their work. In Bay City ES, the data team, which includes teachers and a teaching assistant, plays a central role in monitoring students' progress school-wide. The team uses what is commonly referred to as a data binder in which data culled through two commercial assessment systems are collected and compiled throughout the year. The data team provides guidance and assistance to their colleagues in analyzing and using the data.

Similarly, grade-level teams in Julesberg MS reported poring over items on their benchmark assessments (given three times a year) to identify what specific standards may not be met and by which students: "Our grade-level teams come together and create the test – give it the same day and do item analysis," reported a teacher.

The overall approach can be presented as a developmental sequence: (1) specific areas in need of improvement are identified, down to the unit; (2) new ways of approaching and crafting instruction in that area are designed, implemented, and tested; and (3) student progress is continually assessed. This sequence is a hallmark of the evidence-informed instructional processes in the odds-beating schools. Using disciplined inquiry to drive improvement is one of the ways in which educators in odds-beating schools are enacting the habits of a learning organization.

Significantly, this sequence derives from a set of clear expectations regarding how teachers are expected to work together. A district administrator from Roaring Gap MS shared these expectations, including the conditions needing to be in place. She emphasized the importance of creating a trusting climate for frank discussions about data, setting expectations that data and the dialogues around them should result in action, and providing protocols and routines for these data dialogues to occur.

Leaders in odds-beating schools set the stage for these data dialogues by sending the message that the discussions themselves would be framed by protocols that encourage transparency, authenticity, and actionable outcomes. As the principal at Hutch Hill MS explained,

It's about teaching teachers how to look at data in a very objective way, putting biases aside, and having roles in a group. That school-based inquiry process I believe has been instrumental because the teachers know, "This isn't about me; this is truly looking at how the kids did and who is doing well and who needs help. What seem to be the patterns, what could the interventions be? Okay, let's try these interventions for the next two weeks, now we're going to come back together."

Completion of the document guiding PLC data discussions at Hutch Hill, excerpted in Figure 6.2, is followed by several follow-up questions that prompt team members to reflect on their observations and what adjustments or discussions about instruction need to occur in response to the results. Questions include:

- Are people willing to share their ideas and strategies?
- Once you have identified a question or concept that appears to be better understood by one group of students, what was the teaching strategy or strategies that were used for the most successful group?
- Were you able to share this strategy with the PLC? Are you willing to try this strategy?

Other areas the PLC is prompted to report on are adjustments to curriculum, assessments, resource needs, and factors impacting individual students.

In sum, the kinds of data that are generated, how they are made available, and how they are discussed and used are all important components of the DDI systems in odds-beating schools.

Data Lead Presentation

How can we build/cultivate teacher leadership, accurately assess Common Core curriculum, and use data to inform instruction and adjust curriculum?

Starting the second five weeks of Quarter 3, each course taught will be asked to have at least one summative assessment (graded) and one formative assessment (not graded).

The assessments and the results from the assessments will be coordinated and collected by the Data Lead. The Data Lead will be established by the PLC. The Data Lead will be responsible for the following:

1. Organizing the PLC to select or develop the formative and summative assessments that will be turned in to the department chairperson to submit the assessments to the building principal.
2. Facilitate the PLC discussions in order to complete the Assessment Worksheet.
3. Submit the worksheets to the department chairperson.

Who are the Data Leads? They can be any member of the PLC that is not a Department Chair or a Common Core Leader.

Figure 6.2. Hutch Hill Data Team Guide

Differentiation Strategies

Marks of differentiation in the schools studied were evident in the materials (e.g., texts of different complexity), groupings (e.g., independent, small, or large groupings), types of tasks (e.g., those based on texts versus experience or activity), routines (e.g., use of hand signals and norms/expectations for participation), pacing, and assessments used.

Focusing first on the elementary schools in the study, in a third-grade Yellow Valley class, reading materials of great variety in complexity were selected and presented to children, the teacher keeping in mind the import of balancing both motivation to read and such concerns as lexile levels indicated in the Common Core standards (Williamson, Fitzgerald, & Stenner, 2014). Some students were reading novels, while others were reading short picture books (e.g., *The True Story of the 3 Little Pigs*). In a fifth-grade ELA class, students worked in groups based on their choice of books, and the books were of varying length and complexity.

Likewise, at odds-beating Spring Creek, researchers observed differentiation strategies in use during a fourth-grade math class. Students in that class worked in learning centers where activities were geared to the needs of each group. Some students were doing simple division; others, fractions; and the most advanced group was working on improper fractions using a computer program. The learning center activities involved dice, playing cards, and play-money.

Classroom observations in the odds-beating middle schools found teachers using strategies such as those mentioned earlier, along with providing options in tasks and materials, scaffolding for struggling students, and supplemental guidance, specifically for English language learners and students with disabilities. Moreover, the classrooms can be characterized as inviting and fun—a subjective, yet tangible characteristic of classroom climate as discussed next.

Overall, teachers in the odds-beating schools pay close attention to individual students and endeavor to interact with their interests and needs when possible. They identify struggling students as they are teaching and provide extra scaffolding to move those students in the right direction, or just employ pregnant pauses to allow all students time to think through their responses and have an opportunity to participate.

Classroom observations in these schools revealed that teachers are actively engaged in attempting to provide children the appropriate level of support and challenge as they engage in Common Core-aligned content. They were observed rotating around their classrooms frequently (as opposed to standing at the front of the room or sitting at their desks) and encouraging students to relate their understandings to new content and skills using techniques such as metacognitive questioning (see Kiemer et al., 2015).

Following is a summary description from researchers' observations at Ruby MS that captures the flavor of the classrooms in the odds-beating schools in this regard:

> All of the teachers were very attentive to student responses. All student responses were greeted with a positive and affirming response from the teacher. When students provided responses that seemed beyond what they should know (by grade level) the classroom teacher was quick to probe them for how they came up with their responses. When students explained the origins of their knowledge and understanding, teachers affirmed that their understandings reflected their prior knowledge and experience and were valued.

In contrast, the observations in typical schools yielded high variability in the use of differentiation techniques from classroom to classroom—some in which no differentiation strategies were evident. In addition, responses to interview and focus group questions revealed a pattern among educators in the typically performing schools in relation to challenges to differentiating. They reported needing more planning time and expressed low levels of confidence in knowing how to differentiate the state's ready-made Common Core curriculum modules.

Teachers in the typically performing schools showed a relatively stronger emphasis on preparing children for upcoming assessments through test-like tasks rather than encouraging student discussion of relationships of content to their prior experience. This focus, teachers explained, was related to a perceived or real need to keep all students on pace with an overly ambitious curriculum. A teacher from one typically performing school captured this sentiment in her statement: "The assessment in April shapes what I am going to teach."

In the typically performing schools, higher-performing students were observed being given "busy work" (e.g., find a book and read it until other students are finished), rather than being offered differentiated tasks or materials to extend their learning.

Supplemental Guidance for English Language Learners (ELLs) and Students with Disabilities

Some teachers who are bilingual and able to translate into students' home language held an advantage in successfully engaging ELLs in classroom activities. Urban, linguistically diverse, and odds-beating Julesberg and Sage City middle schools employ bilingual teachers, and these teachers not only use the languages of their students but also a variety of technologies to help display and explain complex content in different ways. Such tactics were not observed in typically performing Silver City MS, which also serves many ELLs.

In Sage City, for example, a bilingual math teacher began class with a count-down in Spanish and then directed students to go to an online math game portal. With school-issued iPads or their own iPhones at the ready, students responded to a fast-paced math quiz that the teacher translated from English into Spanish and displayed on her smart board. The teacher could see which students responded and how, and at times she shared her view with students to recognize the class when all students got the correct answer. Following is an excerpt of the classroom interactions.

> *T:* The question: Which is not a method for solving a system of equations? (T. translates this into Spanish.)
>
> *T:* Elana (a pseudonym) was the first one to get the question!
>
> Students clap excitedly.
>
> *T:* (Again translating into Spanish) Question 2: When the lines intersect, the system has: no solution, one solution, infinite solutions?

After a few seconds the answer comes up on the screen and students again clap. Between each question and answer, students discuss the problem and clap if their answers are correct. The teacher offers some explanation of each of the answers. The questions continue, and during her explanations, the students monitor each other. If students are not listening to the teacher and are talking over her during her explanations, other students quiet them. In general, they are attentive and on task. They are animated and congratulatory when the results come up on their iPhones or iPads and the smart board.

In another example from Julesberg, a classroom teacher (T1) and ESL teacher (T2) work in tandem. They provide different reading materials to engage all students, including the several ELLs, in the same lesson discussing lyrics to a song that will be compared to a poem later in the lesson.

> *T2:* What does it mean if you make allowance—reads aloud—
>
> *T1:* I don't see anyone underlining.
>
> *T2:* What does the line "don't deal in lies" mean? How would you explain it? Any thoughts?
>
> *T1:* So do you know what that means—don't deal in lies?
>
> *S:* Means don't lie.
>
> *T2:* Yeah—don't get involved. OK. What does it mean "don't give way to hating?"

S: I think it means that if people hate you don't hate them back.

T1: Yes—excellent.

T1: (directing students to do a think-pair-share activity) Just talk about your favorite line that matches being a good honest person

Special education teachers in Julesberg also used a variety of techniques to engage and promote student learning. For example, they provided scaffolding by giving step-by-step directions when needed or using visual signals such as a stop sign reminding students to stop and think. They also made regular use of iPads and the apps on them (e.g., dictionary and individualized programs such as eSpark) to scaffold appropriately. According to an Academic Intervention Services (AIS) teacher, "[The iPad] allows students [with disabilities] to be more independent with their own instruction and helps them to become better readers and learners."

Focus on Self-Regulation and Higher-Order Thinking

Another, yet less marked, contrast between instruction in odds-beating and typically performing schools is the focus on fostering students' self-regulation and higher-order thinking skills (i.e., critical, logical, reflective, metacognitive, and creative). In some cases, the attention to developing student's higher-order thinking skills and keeping expectations high in this regard for all students is supported by a clear district vision, as discussed in Chapter 4. For example, one district administrator explained,

> My vision would be that the classroom is operating at the highest level. Students are responsible for their learning, and the teacher is seen as a facilitator so that students can take ownership over their own learning. The teacher would have a positive attitude about those students.

I would want to ensure that when I went into the classroom that the teacher wasn't disparaging of the students, saying they can't do that and complaining about the students who were placed in front of her. I think that attitude is the most critical component of student success, because if you don't believe in your students, they're not going to believe in themselves.

In the schools where the research team observed this emphasis on higher-order thinking, teachers were using self- and peer-assessment techniques to support self-regulation. Teachers posed "What if . . ." questions (i.e., thought experiments) and prompted students to explain their processes for solving problems (in math) or generating conclusions based on analyses of different texts (in ELA).

For example, in a Goliad third-grade ELA class, students were engaged in a writing activity to compare and contrast characteristics of different kinds of frogs as part of a state curriculum module (a bull frog and their own fictional "freaky frog" were the characters). The teacher explained that the purpose of the lesson was to prepare students to compare animals. They engaged in a close read for specific information (e.g., physical characteristics and prey) and wrote comparison/contrast paragraphs on frogs.

Finally, students were directed to write a paragraph that included "vivid words and phrases" and to use "accurate facts" in their descriptions. Here the instructional emphasis was on academic vocabulary and text-to-text interpretations, and children were encouraged to share their drafts with each other.

Engaging and Inclusive Classroom Climates

Although most educators in both odds-beating and typically performing schools expressed a concern with creating a safe and fun environment in their classrooms and schools, it was the odds-beating schools that displayed an emphasis on both cognitive and emotional engagement. This was evidenced in administrators' and teachers' descriptions of what they strive for as well as what was observed in classrooms.

As an instructional coach in Bay City ES said in describing what high-quality instruction looks like in her school, "I really think it's when all the kids are actively engaged. It's very hard; we cannot always have a hundred percent. Sometimes they're not feeling well; sometimes, something happens at home in the morning. . . . But it's having the kids be actively engaged."

Engagement was promoted through the use of classroom norms and procedures so that students understood that they were expected to participate actively in learning. It was also evidenced in teachers' focus on pushing students to their own individual potentials, and this related to the kinds of differentiation techniques they enacted, as described earlier. Teachers also engaged students by celebrating accomplishments throughout their lessons and in instituting a variety of routines to acknowledge exceptional effort and excellent behaviors.

In Starling Springs ES, for example, highly engaging and interactive ELA lessons also integrated history and geography. In one, a fifth-grade student offered a slide presentation he had developed about Bulgarian culture. This elicited comments and questions from both teachers and fellow students. When the student's parent joined him at the front of the class to share a bit of what it had been like growing up in Bulgaria, questions became more animated. For example, students wanted to know about any changes in Bulgaria when it left the Soviet Union and they related Soviet occupation to that of other occupations they knew about (e.g., Japan of Korea).

A Goliad ES teacher attributed her practice of integrating supplementary material and content in her class to the support of reading specialists and mentors who helped with implementing the Common Core standards in ELA. These practices and materials served to bridge the gap between students' background knowledge and the required content in the state's Common Core curriculum modules.

Due to the number of ELLs in Goliad's community, the district had made special efforts to break down and modify the modules for this student group. ESL and ELA teachers at Goliad revise and adapt the modules collaboratively to make them more relevant and accessible to ELLs. Moreover, because of students' language needs, ESL teachers said that they did not rely solely on the modules for instructional material. Rather, they introduced other books and novels to their ELLs and used student-centered instructional strategies such as pair-share and "turn and talk."

Most of the classrooms observed in the odds-beating middle schools were characterized by an inviting, safe, and fun atmosphere, as described in more detail in the case in point. Students showed no fear of speaking up or making mistakes. Teachers used a lot of humor to engage students or called upon them frequently to offer thoughtful responses. In some of the observed classes, students showed authentic enjoyment and ownership of their learning. For example, in Roaring Gap, students expressed hungry excitement to get feedback on their responses and celebrated with claps and hooting when answers were correct.

Likewise, in an ELA class at Julesberg, students begged the teacher to continue with a reading activity saying, "One more, please!" The teacher reminded students of the first day of school: "You said you'd rather go to the dentist than read a book, and I told you that you'll love reading in this class."

In a math class, also in Julesberg, the teacher elicited students' responses by asking, "How do we get out of here?" while making a calculator mistake on purpose. "I'm scared!" he said, and that made a student quickly answer with an explanation, "Don't worry. I'll teach you." The student then proceeded to explain how to use the digital calculator. At Laribee, a teacher tossed the smart board pen around the room to get students to raise their hands and participate in underlining key parts of a problem. Great pace and excitement were evidenced in these classrooms.

Meanwhile in the classrooms observed in the typically performing schools, the climate was generally more traditional, both teacher and assessment centered. When students were off track, teachers either lost them or warned them about repercussions rather than using humor and redirection.

A CASE IN POINT–BAY CITY ELEMENTARY SCHOOL

"You can see what a dangerous animal might be doing." "It won't scare animals away." And "You can see what it does, how it lives when no one is watching." These were among fifth-grade student responses to a teacher question about why researchers used a remote camera to study wildlife as their ELA class prepared to engage in a "close read" of a documentary video, *Great Bear Rainforest Remote Camera Project*, one of a series of informational texts students examined.

Soon, they were busy writing and sharing gist statements as they watched and listened to seven one-minute segments of the video: "Like paragraphs in an article," one student explained. "I'm really impressed. You are doing an awesome job. You're focused and able to identify key ideas from a video," their teacher said as she concluded the lesson.

"I really did think the lesson went well," she reflected later, noting that students responded well to the minor adaptations she had made to the scripted lesson plan and the preparation she had put into the technical aspects of the presentation. "Using informational texts is a big shift. This [state curriculum] module brings in all the standards of the Common Core, including context clues and higher vocabulary," she commented.

This description of an observed lesson provides an example of how Bay City teachers approach instruction. The interviews, focus group discussions, classroom observations, and supporting documents collected produced evidence that educators were working to align curricula and instructional practices with the Common Core State Standards, and they were using a variety of differentiation techniques and student engagement strategies while doing so.

Some of the instructional strategies used to engage students include teacher whole-group facilitation, small group activities, pairing, coteaching, student-led whole-group discussion, student use of white boards and smart boards, one-on-one conferencing, clickers, and hand signaling. Teachers and instructional leaders indicated that engaging students was a top priority in every classroom. Several teachers noted that they were adopting the new strategies as a result of professional development in implementing the CCSS, although they were quick to point out that they had always focused on student engagement.

When asked about the characteristics of high-quality instruction, teachers named differentiation as critical. The art of keeping students involved and interested was seen by teachers as a component of high-quality instruction and an expectation of their peers and administrators.

The district philosophy of "learning for all . . . whatever it takes" is highly aligned with practices and processes at both school and district levels. District leaders have invested financial and material resources into improving instruction and achievement of students in service of their shared vision. District-wide investment in instructional coaches, principals as instructional leaders, building-based substitute teachers, professional development to encourage differentiated instructional strategies, and continuous professional development advance the district aim of offering excellent instruction and maintaining high expectations for student achievement. (Case in Point from Wilcox et al., 2014)

SUMMARY

Odds-beating schools were distinctive in having an evidence-guided system that facilitates the regular use of a variety of data to inform instruction and that allows instructional staff access to useful data on demand. In addition, teachers in these schools had generally well-established, understood, and enacted differentiated instructional strategies at their disposal and were reflexive in their instruction as they analyzed and used data to inform modifications in the classroom.

In addition, educators in odds-beating schools not only reported but also exhibited in their practice the importance of developing independent learners and those who can engage in higher-order thinking by using such techniques as self-questioning and peer assessment. In this way, educators in odds-beating schools demonstrated an emphasis on engaging students cognitively and affectively. Through both the integration of interesting content and the rigor of academic activities, students in the odds-beating schools were actively engaged in learning.

Finally, teachers benefited from school-wide established organizational routines, expectations, and norms to support nurturing an engaging classroom climate and to collaborate with one another around necessary instructional modifications.

As a whole, the ability of educators to effectively change their instructional practices to meet new demands relied heavily upon (1) having proactively worked to develop and use systems that could provide accurate data to inform interventions and instructional adaptations and (2) anticipating the Common Core standards and related innovations (e.g., DDI) and consequently providing both the technical support (e.g., professional development on what the standards are and how to teach to them) and emotional support to deal with the complex and uncertain work of trying new strategies and using new materials in the classroom.

In these ways, the odds-beating schools exemplified systems that engage in improvement principles of adjusting their work to particular problems of practice and making these adjustments user-centered for both teachers and students. Educators in the odds beaters also focused attention on variations in performance as evidenced by their emphasis on data and differentiation. In addition, their data systems facilitated enactment of other improvement principles, namely, seeing the system that produced the outcomes through measurement. In this effort, teachers in the odds-beating schools were engaging in rigorous testing and retesting of how their instructional adaptations were working. In these ways, teachers modeled the improvement science principle of using disciplined inquiry to get better at getting better.

REFERENCES

Allington, R.L. (2010). Recent federal education policy in the United States. In D. Wyse., R. Andrews., & J. Hoffman. (Eds.), *The Routledge International Handbook Series*, (pp. 496–507). New York: Routledge.

Angelis, J.I., & Wilcox, K.C. (2011). Poverty, performance, and frog ponds: What best-practice research tells us about their connections. *Phi Delta Kappan*, 93(3), 26. doi:10.1177/003172171109300307

Baard, S.K., Rench, T.A., & Kozlowski, S. (2014). Performance adaptation: A theoretical integration and review. *Journal of Management*, 40(1), 48–99. doi: 10.1177/0149206313488210

Bryk, A., Gomez, L., Grunow, A., & LeMahieu, P. (2015). *Learning to improve: How America's schools can get better at getting better*. Cambridge, MA: Harvard Education Press.

Cohen, D.K., & Moffitt, S.C. (2009). *The ordeal of inequality: Did federal regulation fit schools?* Cambridge, MA: Harvard University Press.

Darling-Hammond, L. (2010). *The flat world and education: How America's commitment to equity will determine our future*. NY: Teachers College Press.

Datnow, A., & Hubbard, L. (2015). Teachers' use of assessment data to inform instruction: Lessons from the past and prospects for the future. *Teachers College Record*, 117(4).

Fullan, M. (2006). *Turnaround leadership*. San Francisco: Jossey-Bass, Wiley Imprint.

Fullan, M., Rincón-Gallardo, S., & Hargreaves, A. (2015). Professional capital as accountability. *Educational Policy Analysis Archives*, 23(15), 1–18.

Hargreaves, A., & Fullan, M. (2012). *Professional capital: Transforming teaching in every school*. New York: Teachers College Press.

Hiebert, E.H. (2006). Becoming fluent: Repeated reading with scaffolded texts. In S.J. Samuels & A.E. Farstrup (Eds.), *What research has to say about fluency instruction* (pp. 204–226). Newark, DE: International Reading Association.

Honig, M.I., & Venkateswaran, N. (2012). School–central office relationships in evidence use: Understanding evidence use as a systems problem. *American Journal of Education*, 118(2), 199–222. doi:10.1086/663282

Honigsfeld, A., & Dove, M.G. (2012). *Coteaching and other collaborative practices in the EFL/ESL classroom: Rationale, research, reflections, and recommendations.* Charlotte, NC: Information Age Publishing, Inc.

Jundt, D.K., Shoss, M.K., & Huang, J.L. (2014). Individual adaptive performance in organizations: A review. *Journal of Organizational. Behavior,* 36(1), 53–71. doi:10.1002/job.1955

Kiemer, K., Gröschner, A., Pehmer, A. K., & Seidel, T. (2015). Effects of a classroom discourse intervention on teachers' practice and students' motivation to learn mathematics and science. *Learning and Instruction,* 35, 94–103.

Knapp, M.S., Honig, M.I., Plecki, M., Portin, B. & Copland, M. (2014). *Learning-focused leadership in action: Improving instruction in schools and districts.* New York: Routledge.

Council of Chief State School Officers (CCSSO) & The National Governors Association (NGA). (2010). *Common Core State Standards for mathematics and English language arts and literacy in history/social studies, science, and technical subjects. Appendix A.* Washington, DC: National Governors Association. Available at http://www.corestandards.org/assets/Appendix_A.pdf

National Reading Panel. (2000). *Teaching children to read: An evidence-based assessment of the scientific research literature on reading and its implications for reading instruction.* Washington, DC: U.S. Department of Health and Human Services. Retrieved from http://www.nichd.nih.gov/publications/nrp/smallbook. htm.

Olson, C.B., Scarcella, R., & Matuchniak, T. (2015). English learners, writing, and the Common Core. *The Elementary School Journal,* 115(4), 570–592. doi:10.1086/681235

Reis, S.M., McCoach, D.B., Little, C.A., Muller, L. M., & Kaniskan, R. B. (2011). The effects of differentiated instruction and enrichment pedagogy on reading achievement in five elementary schools. *American Educational Research Journal,* 48(2), 462–501. doi:10.3102/0002831210382891

Spillane, J.P. (2012). Data in practice: Conceptualizing the data-based decision-making phenomena. *American Journal of Education,* 118(2), 113–141. doi:10.1086/663283

Wehmeyer, M.L., Field, S., Doren, B., Jones, B., & Mason, C. (2004). Self-determination and student involvement in standards-based reform: Innovative practices. *Exceptional Children,* 70(4), 413–425. doi:10.1177/10983007040060010501

Wilcox, K.C., Durand, F.T., Schiller, K.S., Gregory, K. Zuckerman, S., Felicia, N., Angelis, J.I., & Lawson, H. (2014). *Odds-beating elementary school cross-case report.* Prepared for the New York State Education Department as part of the School Improvement Study. Albany, NY: State University of New York.

Wilcox, K.C., Lawson, H.A., & Angelis, J.I. (2015). Classroom, school and district impacts on minority student literacy achievement. *Teachers College Record,* 117(10). Retrieved from http://www.tcrecord.org/content.asp?contentid=18049

Williamson, G.L., Fitzgerald, J., & Stenner, A.J. (2014). Student reading growth illuminates the Common Core text-complexity standard. *The Elementary School Journal,* 115(2), 230–254. doi:10.1086/678295

York-Barr, J., Ghere, G., & Sommerness, J. (2007). Collaborative teaching to increase ELL student learning: A three-year urban elementary case study. *Journal of Education for Students Placed at Risk*, 12(3), 301–335. doi: 10.1080/10824660701601290.

Ysseldyke, J., Nelson, J.R., Christenson, S., Johnson, D.R., Dennison, A., Triezenberg, H., & Hawes, M. (2004). What we know and need to know about the consequences of high-stakes testing for students with disabilities. *Exceptional Children*, 71(1), 75–95. doi:10.1177/001440290407100105

Chapter Seven

Whole Child Wellness and Positive Youth Development

Karen Gregory, Kristen Campbell Wilcox, and Hal A. Lawson

The requirement that *all* students meet the Common Core State Standards and that teachers and principals be judged on the extent to which they do provides an opportunity for educators to take stock of underlying challenges. Among these challenges are swelling numbers of diverse students arriving at school house doors.

Many of these students face a powerful combination of poverty, social exclusion, challenging home and neighborhood environments, and the effects of abrupt transitions associated with recent immigration. Some of them, while benefiting from their multilingual competencies and rich prior cultural experiences from having lived outside of the United States, nevertheless, may struggle with academic English demands and curricula that assume all children share similar cultural and historical backgrounds that inform their learning.

All such students bring with them a host of needs beyond learning the skills and content of the Common Core. With the link between a child's prior experiences, social and emotional well-being, and academic performance well established (e.g., Durlak, Weissberg, Dymnicki, Taylor, & Schellinger, 2011; Zins, 2004; Zins & Elias, 2007), meeting these needs places new demands on educators, among them the need to reach out to parents and to support families.

Some do this (see, for example, Ishimaru & Lott, 2014; Mapp & Kuttner, 2014), but in reality, many educators have not been professionally prepared to forge relationships with vulnerable parents and families or with community social and health service agencies. Yet the more challenges children bring with them to school, the more apparent the necessity for educators to assume responsibility for addressing needs that had earlier been considered outside educators' domain (Farrington et al., 2012; Moore, 2014).

Poverty-related challenges and obstacles to social inclusion often become barriers to students' healthy development, attendance, engagement, positive behavior, learning, and academic achievement (Angelis & Wilcox, 2011; Lawson & van Veen, 2016). And there is no end to these challenges in sight, as child and family poverty continues to increase in tandem with cultural and ethnic diversity (US Census Bureau, 2016).

In fact, the fastest-growing segment of the early childhood population (5 years old or younger) comes from impoverished and culturally and linguistically diverse families, which schools and public sector health and social services agencies have served least effectively (Annie E. Casey Foundation, 2011). Echoing what children say in hide-and-seek: "Ready or not, here they come."

Clearly, responsive programs and interventions are needed to secure desirable student outcomes and contribute to overall school effectiveness in these turbulent times. Since the odds-beating schools featured in this book serve significant numbers of economically disadvantaged and a growing number of ethnically and linguistically diverse students, they are instructive as others attempt to adapt to new innovations in this increasingly diverse milieu.

This chapter focuses on two questions: What do educators in the odds-beating schools do to address barriers to social inclusion, and healthy social and emotional development while supporting academic learning? How do odds beaters and typical performers vary in their approaches to these barriers?

These two questions structure the ensuing discussion, which first offers an overview of some of the alternatives presented in the research literature about social and emotional development. The discussion then turns to the strategies for integrating culturally responsive practices and supporting social and emotional development found in the odds beaters, with selective contrasts with typical schools.

BEYOND ACADEMICS: THE LANDSCAPE OF MEETING CHILDREN'S NEEDS IN SCHOOLS

As human migration continues to increase and families seek out communities that offer good employment options and good schools for their children, poverty and diversity are no longer seen as primarily an urban school issue (Adelman & Taylor, 2015). Inner-ring suburban and rural schools are also witnessing shifts in their student populations (Tate, 2012).

In contrast to urban schools, many of which have prior experience with, and greater capacity for, meeting comprehensive student and even family needs, suburban and rural schools confront a steep learning curve as they develop new capacities and marshal the resources necessary to address new needs (Lawson, Alameda-Lawson, Lawson, Briar-Lawson, & Wilcox, 2014).

Among educators who seek to expand schools' role to address these needs, academic and social-emotional learning are seen as interrelated; together they have the potential to produce people who learn and achieve at high levels and also demonstrate good character and resilience. This learning is further enhanced by taking a culturally responsive and sustaining approach—one that is intended "to perpetuate and foster linguistic, literate, and cultural pluralism as part of the democratic project of schooling" (Paris, 2013, p. 93).

Schools both in the United States and abroad, including the odds beaters in the study reported here, take one or more of three predominant approaches to fostering student social and emotional development in culturally responsive ways: social and emotional learning programming, coordination of student support services, and mechanisms and structures to encourage whole child wellness. Each of these is discussed in the next section and further illustrated in the findings that follow.

Social and Emotional Learning Programming

Studies structured to examine the effects of appropriately designed and implemented school-based social and emotional learning (SEL) programs indicate that they yield several desirable outcomes. For example, they enhance students' connections to school; improve attitudes about themselves, other people, and the school; enhance social skills and classroom behavior; help to alleviate emotional stress and depression; and reduce problems involving aggression (Durlak et al., 2011; Hamedani & Darling-Hammond, 2015).

In fact, Durlak and colleagues (2011) found that SEL programs are associated with an 11 percentile gain in academic performance. These researchers suggest that four SEL-related factors account for the gains:

1. Peer and adult norms that convey high expectations and support for academic success;
2. Caring teacher–student relationships that foster commitment and bonding to school;
3. Engaging teaching approaches (e.g., proactive classroom management and cooperative learning); and
4. Safe and orderly environments that encourage and reinforce positive classroom behavior (p. 418).

Social and emotional learning programs thus fit and strengthen the conventional focus on teaching and learning.

Student Support Services

The greater the number of ethnically and linguistically diverse students and students growing up in poverty, the greater the number of barriers to attendance, engagement, and learning, and the more schools and districts need systems for well-coordinated student support services (Adelman & Taylor, 2006; Kerr, Dyson, & Raffo, 2014). In some schools, these services are structured to address so-called noncognitive factors that become barriers to learning (Farrington et al., 2012). In others, they involve evidence-based, comprehensive, integrated student support services (Moore, 2014).

In yet others, the idea of comprehensive systems of learning supports has gained traction (Adelman & Taylor, 2006). Learning supports are comprehensive when they encompass the full range of student needs, enabling educators to identify and respond to nearly every conceivable barrier to student attendance, engagement, appropriate behavior, and academic learning. Additionally, learning support systems are comprehensive when they are planned conjointly with community-owned and -operated programs and services.

Whole Child Wellness and Positive Youth Development

Elementary school educators have long been concerned with "whole child" wellness (i.e., social, emotional, physical, and cognitive), and they learn how to help children develop a sense of attachment to them as well as a sense of connection to school. The typical elementary school day in most U.S. public schools has been structured to meet the holistic needs of young children, while facilitating their academic engagement.

Recess is a prime example. It provides an important alternative to often sedentary, academic learning, facilitating children's social and emotional learning while providing physical outlets for young energy, all in support of positive behavior and aiming for transfer into classrooms and beyond.

Subject-centered middle schools have had to take deliberate steps to address whole-child well-being (often named positive youth development) for their preadolescent and early adolescent students (Kieffer, Marinell, & Neugebauer, 2014). This is especially so as pressures have mounted for better test scores, and research shows that academic performance in middle school, together with better counseling, helps to predict college admissions and success (Bowen, Chingos, & McPherson, 2009; Rosenbaum, Deil-Amen, & Person, 2006).

Middle school educators can turn to two kinds of directives for guidance. One is an inventory of optimal practices with middle schoolers. Typically, these lists include the following priorities:

- A sense of connection to school;
- A sense of attachment to a least one caring adult at school, ideally a teacher;
- Membership in one or more peer groups with prosocial orientations;
- Voice, choice, and leadership opportunities;
- Personalization in classrooms and schools overall; and
- Harmonized home, community, and school environments, evidenced by shared norms, expectations, and behavioral rules (Blum, 2005; Mitra, 2007; Nagaoka, Farrington, Ehrlich, & Heath, 2016).

These recommended practices become stronger when they are combined with the recommended features of middle schools as organizations, such as those published by the Association for Middle Level Education (2010). These features include:

- Comprehensive guidance and support services for young adolescents;
- A safe, inviting, inclusive and supportive environment for everyone;
- Support for health and wellness in curricula, school-wide programs, and related policies;
- Active involvement with families, community, and business partners; and
- Organizational structures to foster purposeful learning and meaningful relationships (p. 21).

SOCIAL AND EMOTIONAL DEVELOPMENT IN ODDS-BEATING SCHOOLS

Educators in odds-beating schools embrace an inclusive, holistic stance toward children and youths. During interviews, they stated their firm belief that young people perform better academically when they are healthy and feel included, safe, secure, and happy. These educators emphasized how they strive to care for, connect with, and engage all children in culturally responsive ways. Significantly, many referred to "our kids" and "our students," that is, they used possessive language that expressed their deep feelings and firm commitments to the young people in their care.

As discussed in Chapter 2, school climate plays a key role in providing a supportive organizational context for both children and adults to engage in this kind of caretaking. A supportive and collaborative work environment hinges on relations among all participants—adults with adults (including in the community), adults with students, and students with students. A school climate survey administered as part of this study revealed that respondents in odds-beating schools were more likely than those in typically performing schools to agree that students get along with each other and are generally respectful to adults.

When a critical mass of educators in a school agree that social and emotional well-being is a priority and have made strides to realize its potential by embedding it in organizational structures, social and emotional development becomes a systemic feature. The odds beaters in this study are defined, in part, by the structures, routines, and environments that educators within them are striving to institutionalize in support of children's social and emotional development and overall well-being (Byrk, Sebring, Allensworth, Luppescu, & Easton, 2009; Durlak et al., 2011).

Although organizational environments may have considerable staying power, they neither grow nor endure automatically. Rather, climate-enhancing, interpersonal relationships are socially constructed in each school and they are adaptive to the children and communities they serve.

Educators in the odds-beating schools demonstrated an ability to work together to steward their schools on behalf of students, yet they often admitted that their work was not done. They provided convincing, realistic appraisals of the challenges they confront, especially those accompanying student poverty (e.g., hunger and mental health needs) and diversity (e.g., social services and student and family English language needs).

In the same vein, some admitted that the special programs and services they currently offer (e.g., finding ways to get students involved in extracurricular activities; forging partnerships with families and communities; instituting a character education program) amount to works in progress, further indicating an adaptive posture as they figure out what works for particular kinds of students. Some were guided in their decisions by data they collected to gauge results and monitor progress.

The following sections provide examples from the odds-beating schools, with contrasts from the typical performers, about practices and programs implemented to address barriers to cultural inclusion and healthy student social and emotional development. Given the greater challenges for middle-level educators to incorporate such practices and programs into the typical middle school structure, the emphasis in this chapter is on the middle school.

The chapter closes with a representative case in point from one elementary school that serves above-average percentages of economically disadvantaged and diverse students.

Culturally Responsive Teaching and Schooling

Students' social and emotional development, including their interpersonal attachments, sense of belonging, peer group affiliations, and sense of connections to school hinge on a variety of school-wide efforts to foster a socially integrated, inclusive community. In these respects, odds beaters overall are selectively different from typical performers and exhibited characteristics of cultural responsiveness.

Odds-beating schools demonstrated that a culturally responsive approach to schooling is an important aspect of system-wide programming for healthy social and emotional development for diverse populations. This approach celebrates diversity, viewing all students as equally valuable, capable, and with varied assets and resources that derive from their richly varied cultural or linguistic backgrounds (Nieto, 2000, 2010; Gay, 2010). Culturally responsive schooling moves toward individualization and differentiation, building upon students' already developed "funds of knowledge" to help them succeed in and outside of school (Moll & Gonzales, 2004).

Some features of a culturally responsive school system include structures to mainstream diverse students through sheltered instruction and coteaching models of instruction (Echevarria, Vogt & Short, 2004; Peercy, 2011, Theoharis & O'Toole, 2011; Wilcox, 2012) and processes to create connections between home and school (Ramirez & Jimenez-Silva, 2014).

A culturally responsive school supports social and emotional wellness by integrating students into extracurricular activities, helping them to achieve academic success in the most inclusive environment, and providing structured and effective assistance for struggling students in and outside of the classroom.

For example, educators at odds-beating Goliad ES worked hard to bridge the gap between students' background knowledge and the required content in the state curriculum modules. They did this by taking students on field trips and providing supplementary reading material relating to students' cultural heritage or lived experiences. Teachers collaborated to revise and adapt the curriculum so that it was more culturally relevant to English learning students and more accessible, considering their language proficiency.

In Starling Springs ES, educators explained that the high number of ELLs (English language learners) prompted the creation of several elementary ESL centers in which services are concentrated. Widespread appreciation for multicultural and multilingual children was expressed by several teachers, with one capturing a prevalent theme: "I love that in any given year there are at least seven different languages spoken at home [among the students] in my classroom." Another exclaimed, "What we learn from our students! [It's] amazing!"

As well as offering culturally responsive instructional strategies, bilingual faculty and staff in odds-beating schools like Julesberg and Sage City middle schools translate documents into students' home languages. This was not reported to be the case in typically performing Silver City MS, which also serves many ELLs.

The inclusionary practices evidenced in the odds beaters are drivers for social and emotional learning and further relate to both school engagement and academic engagement. The best of the odds beaters were exemplars in this regard.

Elements of Comprehensive Systems to Address Students' Needs

In addition to providing culturally responsive approaches particularly important for culturally and linguistically diverse children, odds-beating schools in this study were distinct from typical performers in the systems they put in place to formally support all children's social and emotional development. In several, these systems were propelled by strategies structured to develop better relationships between children and adults, connect students to school through a variety of activities, develop character, integrate academic and social services, and create and sustain partnerships with families and community services.

These efforts were forged as part of an overall plan to address barriers to healthy development, attendance, engagement, positive behavior, and learning. The sections that follow share examples of practices related to each.

Connections between Children and Adults

Turning to the middle schools in this study, educators in the odds beaters made systematic efforts to connect children with adults because they know how important it is to build and sustain positive interpersonal relationships. The principal of Ruby MS summarized the school's rationale:

> I feel our goals are to form relationships with students and to make sure they're comfortable when they're learning and if those two things are happening, then children are going to be successful. If they don't have a relationship with somebody and they're not comfortable where they sit, then they're not going to be productive learners.

Educators at Ruby have supportive resources and the guidance provided by their own data systems, including results of a survey of every student in the middle school about their interests, hobbies, and opinions regarding the operation of the school. Student responses to this survey are used to help the principal, teachers, and support staff to develop stronger connections to children as well as guide resource allocations.

Hutch Hill provides another example of a school that prioritizes adult–child connections. The school day is structured to cement these relationships. In the principal's words,

We have [an] advisory period . . . [for] a smaller group of students, somewhere between 5 and 7, and . . . we have about 15 minutes every day with that same group of students for three years. It provides us with an opportunity to draw a stronger connection to a smaller group of students and for the students to have a stronger rapport with another faculty person, somebody on staff that they would be comfortable going to if there's an issue or a problem.

A third example comes from Laribee, which also offers a formalized mentoring program for students at risk of failure. A district leader described it in the following way:

So through the counselors, students who may be in need are identified very confidentially and teachers come forth and say, "Yes I'd be interested in being a formal mentor." And so maybe you're connected to me, and I develop a relationship with you and maybe you're a 7th grader and we develop a relationship. And maybe you come in at lunchtime and we have lunch together and I help you with your homework or just check in in the morning, or some activities . . . that kind of thing.

In contrast, typically performing schools revealed a less formalized and systematic method of connecting children and adults—a more hit-or-miss approach. In two of the three typically performing middle schools, school leaders and teachers expressed a general awareness of the importance of creating connections between adults and children, but with apparently little attention to how educators would be supported systematically in developing relationships.

In short, in typical performers, differences emerged between educators' espoused beliefs and priorities and the work that actually got done (Argyris & Schön, 1996). For example, the principal at typically performing Locus Glen MS explained a focus on getting "buy in" from kids by putting "staff who want to be here out in the hallway, who want to smile at kids, want to make connections with kids." Clearly, this principal knows the importance of cultivating positive adult–child relationships, but the school has no system in place to ensure that it happens.

School-Sponsored Extracurricular Programs and Activities

In both odds-beating and typically performing schools, educators stated that one way for students and teachers to develop positive relationships is through extracurricular activities. In every school, teachers and administrators described the coaching, mentoring, and club advisement that teachers took part in, and they also described how important that was to students, especially at the middle school level. Considerable research supports the claim that positive outcomes from students' extracurricular involvements translate into improvements in classroom engagement and learning (Eccles & Roesner, 2011; Lawson & Lawson, 2013).

At the elementary level, odds-beating schools offered afterschool enrichment, whereas typical performers were more likely to offer remediation. And at the middle level, while both odds beaters and typical performers prioritized extracurricular activity as a way to keep students engaged and connected to school, the odds beaters facilitated participation with supports such as afterschool busing and paid stipends for teachers.

The superintendent for odds-beating Hutch Hill described why extracurricular activities are so important for all students, but especially for the neediest students in the population:

> Band, chorus, orchestra, art, athletics. We're increasing all of that because at the end of the day there's another 2–3 hours that these kids need to have something to do and the best investment—the least expensive investment that a district has in terms of personnel is hiring advisors and coaches for that 2–3 hours at the end of the school day. It occupies kids' time but it also provides the opportunities for a lot of kids to participate in an activity. But it also does this: It puts a positive role model in every child's life.

In Ruby, another odds-beating middle school, teachers described efforts to include *all* students in extracurricular activities. Theirs is a full-inclusion strategy: students are not cut from sports teams or groups like the school orchestra. Instead, educators work to include all and make each feel an important part of the team or group. One teacher said, "But if a kid wants to play football or soccer or be in music or be in the school play or be in band or chorus, or x, y, z—because we're small enough, anyone that wants to be in anything can be in it—cocurricular, extracurricular, it doesn't matter across the board what it is."

Character Education and Positive Behavior Programming

In odds-beating schools, character education and programming to encourage positive behavior is characterized by its prioritization, depth, and locally contextualized design. The research team heard and saw how positive behavior frameworks and character education can have a positive impact on the learning environment of a school when it is systematically implemented. Although the specific strategies and programs varied among schools, odds-beating elementary and middle schools were aligned in their priorities for whole-child development and strategies that yield positive behavior, adult–child connections, and classroom engagement.

In the odds-beating elementary schools, character education and programming to promote positive behavior were considered to be foundational to their success. Examples include anti-bullying programs; whole-school morning meetings; character-building assemblies; support groups for children with family challenges, bereavement, or socialization issues; and systems in place for student and family counseling.

In Bay City ES, for example, the assistant principal spoke about a team approach in which administrators, teachers, counselors, and specialists work together to support struggling students:

> Teachers refer children for several reasons and that's where we really diagnose the child looking at the whole picture. Why is this child not making academic progress? We dig deep into the history of the child, the family, track attendance, whether or not they're on medications. We spend a lot of time getting to know the kids on an individual basis.

And at Yellow Valley ES, character education is central to the philosophy of the school. A building leadership team member described how this philosophy plays a part in decision making at the school: "We follow the 4 B's, be here and ready, be safe, be caring, and be respectful. That's a huge part of our building planning and a huge part around which everything else is based." When needed, a staff member reported, adults are more likely to ask children if they are being safe, etc., rather than making a "don't" statement. In this way, they teach self-regulation.

Several middle schools had a Positive Behavioral Intervention and Supports (PBIS) program in place. A district leader in odds-beating Roaring Gap described how PBIS there is specifically geared for their students, and how students have begun to take leadership over the program as they positively influence one another. He explained, "When they want to learn, they don't want somebody else distracting them. I think because we have done a great job in terms of emulating and showing them what it means to be focused and be ready to learn, to be respectful and responsible, they now do it with each other."

PBIS and character education programs are important aspects of typically performing schools as well, but they were found to be less structured, planned, and formalized. For example, in Tarelton, a more generic system is in place, as described by a building leader:

> When we had grade level meetings, . . .the first thing I said [to the students] was, "Our expectations are focused on three areas: being safe, being respectful, and being responsible." . . . Any time that I have a child that comes in here on a bus referral, on a classroom referral, or a cafeteria referral – I pull that out. I say, "Listen, what expectations did you not meet? Was your behavior safe? Was your

behavior respectful? Was your behavior responsible?" And then I will read it to them again by going through what the expectations for each one of our areas are and then I also have think sheets and behavioral reflections that follow PBIS.

When Tarelton's PBIS program is compared with the one at Roaring Gap, an important, consequential difference becomes evident: A more differentiated, context-specific plan is in place at Roaring Gap, and it is accompanied by a deeper philosophical commitment to the program. A Roaring Gap district leader emphasized the importance of tailoring standardized programs such as PBIS to the local context:

> The lessons have to be different, and we have to differentiate to some extent. There's a portion of PBIS, if the students are behaving the way you expect them to behave, you also have to acknowledge that. . . . That acknowledgement may be different depending on [their maturity]. . . . You [also] have to tailor the lesson where they can truly understand and grasp the concept. So you may do a lesson on perseverance for a 7th or 8th grader, but it may look different. It's still perseverance, but the things that you talk about with a 6th grader may be a little bit unique to what you talk about with an 8th grader.

Taken together, these findings demonstrate how educators in the odds-beating schools act strategically to ensure that their respective character education programs and positive behavior management programs have been explicitly tailored to fit their school and are systematically enacted, articulated among staff, and consistent.

Integrating Academic and Support Services

Programming for social and emotional learning and development requires educators to adapt school structures, procedures, and instruction to meet the needs of all students. Odds-beating schools demonstrate that such design and implementation work is a collective enterprise that hinges on the extent to which educators at all levels of the system are able to work together, whether in formal teams, communities of practice, or strong professional networks.

Most teachers have not received preparation specific to social and emotional development in their preservice education programs, but student support professionals, particularly school psychologists and counselors, have. In schools that prioritize student social and emotional development, the latter often work with teams of classroom teachers and/or side by side with them in classrooms (Moore, 2014; Nagaoka et al., 2016).

In all six odds-beating middle schools in the study, teachers work in collaborative teams that meet regularly to discuss not only curriculum and instruction but also the health and well-being of their shared students. Teachers in all of these schools repeatedly mentioned how important it was to have structured time set aside to discuss students and their needs. In many schools, the support staff, including guidance counselors, social workers, or school psychologists, are either formally part of the teams or collaborate closely with the teams to attend to the social and emotional health of students.

A student support services staff member at Hutch Hill described their formal process of collaborative teaming to support students' social and emotional developmental health:

> We absolutely work as a collaborative team. . . . If we need to involve more resources, then . . . that information is brought by the counselors to the administrators, and we involve other people whether they be service providers or probation officers, and maybe just brainstorming what to do in that group of people. And that group meets once a week. So there are a lot of formal things in place for us to stay connected and stay very current with what's going on with our students.

The principal of Sage City described her school's teaming structure and its benefits to students and families:

> I think the team structure is also a really good structure for parents and kids. So the team will invite the parent in and instead of having to go talk to the English teacher, the math teacher, the science teacher, all meetings are inclusive, so it's the whole team; plus the counselor will come and the psychologist or social worker if necessary. So everyone will sit down with the parent, and the parent can request a meeting at any time throughout the year.

In typically performing middle schools, the research team heard that these types of meetings happened, but less frequently. At Tarelton, for example, a support staff member described working with each grade-level team only once every two weeks.

And in Locus Glen the teaming structure had been dismantled as part of the district's response to budget limitations. Both support staff members and building leaders described some of the resulting losses, including parent conferences and the ability of teachers to collectively discuss student needs. A building leader said regretfully,

> When you had that group of teachers meeting every Monday through Thursday to talk about kids, to hold kids accountable, to see who is struggling where and to make parent phone calls, and have your parent meetings then. . . . It was a great process.

As a result, he continued, faculty and administrators now need to rely more on the school social worker, guidance counselors, and psychologists, leaving teachers uninformed, sometimes, and out of the communication loop.

Academic–social service collaboration in odds-beating schools also includes counselors and support staff working inside the classroom. They often coteach and join teachers to offer direct instruction or workshops on social and emotional developmental issues. Students benefit (Durlak et al., 2011; Lawson & Briar-Lawson, 1997), teachers receive embedded professional development, and connections between teachers and student support professionals facilitate student referrals for specialized, personalized psychological services (e.g., mental health or behavior problems).

For example, the support staff of odds-beating Laribee MS described some of the work they do in classrooms to help prevent bullying and harassment. "Over a two-day period, we do 17 or 18 presentations, the whole population at different times within those two days. . . . It focuses on communication skills, working in groups . . . conflict resolution."

In Sage City, the principal described how the work of counselors and support staff reaches beyond the traditional scope and becomes highly individualized according to the needs of students:

The counselors also do groups . . . they did a six-week group in November, and each counselor chose a different topic. So one, the psychologist, did impulsivity, and she worked with four boys who were very impulsive to sort of get them to think about their impulsive behavior. One of the other counselors worked with seven habits of highly effective teens. And each of the kids was chosen for these groups because they were the right fit.

In Laribee, allocation of resources for support staff demonstrates commitment to social and emotional well-being, as described by an assistant superintendent:

We are fortunate that we have a psychologist in every building plus . . . there's a district psychologist. . . . We meet regularly. [He] goes to every building on a weekly basis . . . so that we have coordination and consistency. He meets with the psychologists. We have guidance counselors, one at each elementary, two at the middle, and eight at the high school, who meet regularly with the director of counseling.

These resources offer a sharp contrast with typically performing Locus Glen, where the district psychologist moves between buildings, restricting the level of care she is able to provide. One staff member said, "If [the matter] is something that is associated with an IEP (Individualized Education Plan) like a behavioral issue, that kind of thing . . . she has to be involved. Because she is split between buildings, she doesn't have the time to do individual stuff as much." Another added, "A lot of what she does is crisis intervention, and if she's only here half the time (laughing), the crisis can only happen when she is here."

The principal of typically performing Tarelton MS also expressed the need for more support staff to share the case load: "I think there's always a need for another counselor, probably in every district. . . . I think it would benefit not only students but staff as well."

In all of the middle schools in the study, staff members in various roles said that they were confronting challenges posed by student poverty and transience and a lack of funding. Faced with these shared challenges, differences were evident between odds-beating and typically performing schools and districts. In odds beaters, a firm, school-level commitment to support the social and emotional development and overall well-being of students was supported and resourced at the district level, in part by funding adequate support staff for the needs of the student population.

Creating and Sustaining Community Partnerships

Another aspect of district-wide priorities and support for students' social, emotional, and mental health was evident in district central office leaders' efforts to reach outside the boundaries of the district in the quest for community partners to offer services, assistance and resources. In contrast to typical performers, the data reveal that creating these partnerships at the district level was prioritized in odds beaters.

In Hutch Hill, for example, the superintendent discussed recent increases in student mental health problems and explained why and how the district is partnering with a local mental health agency to meet the needs of the community. His words demonstrate the systematic approach that distinguished odds-beating from typically performing schools.

> Why don't we bring the services to the children? Where the children are, right here. We bus them to school every day, we take them home every night, let's provide a medical health service for children *on* campus. . . . We're working with [a community agency] to get [it] on campus sometime this fall. We've been working with them for close to a year now, applied for a grant, didn't get the grant, so we'll use local dollars, because it's just too important not to do.

In Ruby MS, the district takes a different approach to partnering; one apparently tailor-made for its context. The support staff described their partnership with an agency that provides wraparound services for families in need. They said that a coordinator from this agency explains all the services that are available to families and works as a liaison between the home and the school:

They take the family and they invite all the people involved with the family, including the school, anybody else, and we come around the table. We talk about strengths; we talk about needs. And then we give everybody a role, including the parent.

Ruby also partners with the county social services department, department of health, substance abuse counselors, youth advocates, the local police, and the town court judge. A teacher described their partnerships this way: "So it's a village. You know that whole saying, 'It takes a village.' We have a village that we invite into our school, because you can't do it alone."

Typically performing Tarelton is also challenged by its population's mental health concerns. Staff there expressed frustration that the district does not have a close connection to community agencies or other community professionals for outside help, saying that in their rural area resources are few and demand is higher than supply. One support staff professional said, in part,

So I'd say the need(s) are not being met, but it's not because of neglect. It's just the sheer fact that there's a high need and it's not just the kids. . . . And sometimes I would say it's even the kids that are more intact than the parents are. That's hard, and it's hard because that is a huge roadblock academically for kids.

Overall, educators in the odds-beating schools were striving to meet the changing needs of their populations by expanding services to serve a wider range of needs and to insure that every student feels connected to the school's academic and extracurricular programs. These expanding priorities required changing roles and relationships within the school (e.g., teachers and student support professionals working together in classrooms), and reaching beyond the school to enlist or contribute to community social service providers.

A CASE IN POINT—GOLIAD ELEMENTARY SCHOOL

Success is knowing that ultimately all that you are doing is for the best interest of the child. . . . When you see children smiling and well adjusted, doing the very best that they can, especially during this very challenging time in education, you know that you have met some measure of success.

—principal

Goliad is an urban elementary school with a diverse student population. Its focus on students' social, emotional, and physical health is tied to educators' belief that children need to be healthy, safe, and secure in order to reach their academic potential. "I would like my children here . . . to be able to have equal access to all that exists for them in this world," the principal said, reflecting a culturally responsive approach to educating all children with equity. A district administrator stated that students' physical and emotional health plays an important role in educating the "whole child" and should be the foundation of academic success.

Student well-being and readiness to learn begin with physical health. A wellness committee promotes healthy food choices and fun ways to exercise during the school day. For example, during "Wellness Week," a different healthy activity is planned for each day; the school has also purchased pedometers to encourage students to walk during recess. The school partners with parents to provide health care for the children. Free glasses are offered to students through the teachers' union vision plan, and free dental care, through the Smiles program. Together, these services make the school a centerpiece of childhood health and wellness management.

Another top priority at the school is student safety. The principal articulated that it is an integral part of the school mission to "supply a very safe and secure learning environment, where our students feel like this building is a safe haven, a home away from home." The district also initiated "Saturday School" to involve parents in discussions about student safety and well-being. Discussions cover several school-related topics chosen to inform parents about ways they can help their children succeed in school.

The support staff at Goliad described the social, physical, and emotional development of students as fundamental to meeting the district's academic goals. The principal articulated that discipline issues had decreased because of constructive behavioral interventions and the proactive measures of the assistant principal, who is responsible for student behavior management.

A culturally responsive approach to instruction creates an atmosphere of equity and inclusion in the classroom. For example, the district has made special efforts to break down and modify the state Common Core-aligned curriculum modules for English learners. English as a Second Language (ESL) and English language arts (ELA) teachers revise and adapt the modules collaboratively to make them more relevant and accessible to ELL students.

Moreover, because of some multilingual students' instructional adaptation needs, ESL teachers do not rely solely on the state's modules or other commercially available programs and products for instructional material. Rather, they introduce multicultural books and novels to their students and use instructional strategies to actively engage students such as pair-share and "turn and talk." For families of English learners, translators are available for meetings, and school mailings are also translated into the various languages spoken by families served by the school.

The school building is designed to encourage collaborative relationships, with many common areas, shared spaces, and fluid walls between classrooms. Both school administrators and teachers described a family-like atmosphere at the school, and many said there was no place else they would enjoy working more. They also described their commitment to creating a safe and warm environment for children and to educating them as "well-rounded" people with social, emotional and physical health, intellectual capability, a humanitarian spirit, and cultural sensitivity. (Case in Point from Wilcox et al., 2014)

SUMMARY

Evidence gleaned in this study indicates that educators in the odds-beating schools prioritize social inclusion and social-emotional development and that they recognize both as necessary to support academic success. They are striving to enact a systematic strategy to support and achieve both. Although their innovation journey in this regard is not done, they have made impressive strides, particularly in comparison with the typical performers.

Like their counterparts in the typical performers, they are acutely aware of changes in their respective student populations and recognize the need for help. Where they differ in this regard is in the extent to which they have developed formal programs, practices, and arrangements as well as new partnerships with community agencies charged with mental health, health, and social services. These arrangements include their collaborative cultures and integration of academic and social services.

They also differ from the typical performers in their focus on social and cultural inclusion for all students. As is recognized by educators in the odds-beating schools, extracurricular activities produce school engagement, and school engagement tracks into academic (classroom) engagement; and vice versa (Lawson & Lawson, 2013). To quote the superintendent of Julesberg, participation gives students "a running start into eventual intellectual gains."

In these several respects and others, odds-beating schools and their district offices differed from most of the typical performers. These differences help to account for odds beaters' comparatively better outcomes.

REFERENCES

Adelman, H.S. & Taylor, L. (2006). *The school leader's guide to student learning supports: New directions for addressing barriers to learning.* Thousand Oaks, CA: Corwin Press.

Adelman, H.S. & Taylor, L. (2015). Immigrant children and youth in the USA: Facilitating equity of opportunity at school. *Education Sciences*, 5, 323–344.

Angelis, J. & Wilcox, K.C. (2012). Poverty, performance, and frog ponds: What best practice research tells us about their connections. *Phi Delta Kappan*, 93(3) 26–31.

Annie E. Casey Foundation (2011). *Kids count data book*. Baltimore, MD: Author.

Argyris C., & Schön, D. (1996). *Organizational learning II: Theory, method and practice*, Reading, MA: Addison Wesley.

Association for Middle Level Education (formerly National Middle School Association) (2010). *This we believe: Keys to educating young adolescents*. Westerville, OH: Author.

Blum, R. (2005). *School connectedness: Improving students' lives*. Baltimore: Bloomberg School of Public Health, Johns Hopkins University.

Bowen, W.G., Chingos, M., & McPherson, M. (2009). *Crossing the finish line: Completing college at America's public universities*. Princeton, NJ: Princeton University Press.

Bryk, A.S., Sebring, P.B., Allensworth, E., Luppescu, S., & Easton, J.Q. (2009). *Organizing schools for improvement: Lessons from Chicago*. Chicago: Chicago University Press.

Durlak, J.A., Weissberg, R., Dymicki, A., Taylor, R., & Schellinger, K. (2011). The impact of enhancing students' social and emotional learning: A meta-analysis of school-based universal interventions. *Child Development*, 82(1), 405–432.

Eccles, J.S., & Roeser, R.W. (2011). Schools as developmental contexts during adolescence. *Journal of Research on Adolescence*, 21(1), 225–241.

Echevarria, J., Vogt, M., & Short, D. (2004). *Making content comprehensible for English learners: The SIOP model*. Boston: Allyn and Bacon.

Farrington, C.A., Roderick, M., Allensworth, E., Nagaoka, J., Keyes, T., Johnson, D., & Beechum, N. (2012). Teaching adolescents to become learners. The role of noncognitive factors in shaping school performance: A critical literature review. Chicago: University of Chicago Consortium on Chicago School Research. Downloaded from: http://ccsr.uchicago.edu/sites/default/files/publications/Noncognitive%20Report.pdf

Gay, G. (2010). *Culturally responsive teaching: Theory, research, and practice*. New York: Teachers College Press.

Hamedani, M. G., & Darling-Hammond, L. (2015). Social emotional learning in high school: How three urban high schools engage, educate, and empower youth. Stanford Center for Opportunity Policy in Education. *March*. Downloaded from: https://edpolicy.stanford.edu/publications/pubs/1310

Ishimaru, A.M., & Lott, J. (2014). *Charting a course to equitable collaboration: Learning from the parent engagement initiatives in the road map project*. Seattle: University of Washington College of Education. Downloaded from: https://education.uw.edu/sites/default/files/research/projects/epsc/EquitableCollaborationReport_0.pdf

Kerr, K., Dyson, A., & Raffo, C. (2014). *Education, disadvantage, and place: Making the local matter*. Chicago: Policy Press.

Kieffer, M.J., Marinell, W.H., & Neugebauer, S.R. (2014). Navigating into, through, and beyond middle grades: The role of middle grades attendance in staying on track for high school graduation. *Journal of School Psychology*, 52, 549–565. doi: 0.1016/j.jsp.2014.09.002

Lawson, H.A., Alameda-Lawson, T., Lawson, M., Briar-Lawson, K., & Wilcox, K.C. (2014). Three parent and family interventions for rural schools and communities. *Journal of Education and Human Development*, 3(3), 59–78. doi: 10.15640/jehd. v3n3a5

Lawson, H., & Briar-Lawson, K. (1997). *Connecting the dots: Progress toward the integration of school reform, school-linked services, parent involvement and community schools*. Oxford, OH: The Danforth Foundation & The Institute for Educational Renewal at Miami University.

Lawson, H.A. & van Veen, D. (2016). *Developing community schools, community learning centers, extended-service, and multi-service schools: International exemplars for practice, policy, and research*. The Hague, NL: Springer International.

Lawson, M.A., & Lawson, H.A. (2013). New conceptual frameworks for student engagement research, policy, and practice. *Review of Educational Research*, 83(3), 432–479. doi:10.3102/0034654313480891

Mapp, K.L., & Kuttner, P.J. (2014). *Partners in education: A dual capacity-building framework for family-school partnerships*. Austin, TX & Washington, DC: SEDL & U.S. Department of Education. Downloaded from: http://www.sedl.org/pubs/framework/

Mitra, D. (2007). The role of administrators in enabling youth-adult partnerships in schools. *NASSP Bulletin*, 91(3), 237–256.

Moll, L.C., & González, N. (2004). Engaging life: A funds of knowledge approach to multicultural education. *Handbook of research on multicultural education*, 2, 699–715.

Moore, K.A. (2014). *Making the grade: Assessing the evidence for integrated student supports*. Bethesda, MD: Child Trends. Downloaded from: http://www. childtrends.org/wp-content/uploads/2014/02/2014-07ISSPaper2.pdf

Nagaoka, J., Farrington, C., Ehrlich, S., & Heath, R. (2016). *Foundations for young adult success: A developmental framework*. Chicago: University of Chicago Consortium on Chicago School Research. Downloaded from: https://consortium.uchicago.edu/publications/foundations-young-adult-success-developmental-framework

Nieto, S. (2010). *Language, culture, and teaching: Critical perspectives*. New York: Routledge.

Nieto, S. (2000). Placing equity front and center: Some thoughts on transforming teacher education for a new century. *Journal of Teacher Education*, 51(3), 180–187.

Paris, D. (2012). Culturally sustaining pedagogy: A needed change in stance, terminology, and practice. *Educational Researcher*, 41(3), 93–97.

Peercy, M.M. (2011). Preparing English language learners for the mainstream: Academic language and literacy practices in two junior high school ESL classrooms. *Reading & Writing Quarterly*, 27(4), 324–362.

Ramirez, P. C., & Jimenez-Silva, M. (2014). Secondary English learners: Strengthening their literacy skills through culturally responsive teaching. *Kappa Delta Pi Record*, 50(2), 65–69.

Rosenbaum, J.E., Deil-Amen, R., & Person, A. (2006). *After admission: From college access to college success*. New York: Russell Sage Foundation.

Tate, W.F. (2012). *Research on schools, neighborhoods, and communities*. Chicago: Rowman & Littlefield Publishers & the American Educational Research Association.

Theoharis, G., & O'Toole, J. (2011). Leading inclusive ELL social justice leadership for English language learners. *Educational Administration Quarterly*, 47(4), 646–688.

United States Census Bureau (2016). Child and family poverty rates 2014. Downloaded from: http://www.census.gov/hhes/www/poverty/

Wilcox, K.C. (2012). Diversity as strength: How higher-performing schools embrace diversity and thrive. In A. Cohan & A. Honigsfeld (Eds.), *Breaking the mold of education for culturally and linguistically diverse students: Innovative and successful practices for the 21st century* (pp. 47–51). New York: Rowman & Littlefield.

Wilcox, K.C., Durand, F.T., Schiller, K.S., Gregory, K., Zuckerman, S., Felicia, N., Angelis, J.I., & Lawson, H. (2014). *Odds-beating elementary school cross-case report*. Prepared for the New York State Education Department as part of the School Improvement Study. Albany, NY: State University of New York.

Zins, J.E. (Ed.). (2004). *Building academic success on social and emotional learning: What does the research say?* New York: Teachers College Press.

Zins, J.E., & Elias, M.J. (2007). Social and emotional learning: Promoting the development of all students. *Journal of Educational and Psychological Consultation*, 17(2–3), 233–255.

Chapter Eight

Odds Beaters as Exemplars

Hal A. Lawson, Kristen Campbell Wilcox, and Janet Ives Angelis

Together the odds-beating schools and district offices that are the subject of this book provide an exemplar. That is, they serve to provide a research-supported model for practice and policy and one that both anticipated and responds to calls for policy innovation implementation research (Coburn, Hill, & Spillane, 2016). These exemplars earn this status for three reasons:

1. They serve relatively high percentages of ethnically and linguistically diverse students and students who are growing up in poverty, yet they achieved above predicted student outcomes.
2. They simultaneously implemented three disruptive policy innovations without short-term performance declines.
3. The innovations penetrated to classrooms, changing what and how teachers teach and what and how students learn.

Why and how were they successful at beating the odds? Like the pieces of a jigsaw puzzle, each of the previous chapters provides a partial answer. This chapter assembles the several pieces, providing, as it were, the picture on the top of the puzzle box. Following the presentation of an overarching policy implementation framework, this concluding chapter provides an integrative summary of the innovation implementation strategies in the odds-beating schools and their districts in tandem with a composite theory of action.

THE INNOVATION IMPLEMENTATION JOURNEY

Innovations such as the Common Core State Standards (CCSS), annual professional performance review (APPR) systems (based, in part, on students'

performance on Common Core assessments), and data-driven instruction
(DDI) are expected to successfully journey from a state education department
policy drawing board to school-level practice at scale. However, much can
happen during the course of this journey, and for this reason, implementation
typically is problematic rather than automatic.

Boundary Theory and Research

Boundary theory and research (e.g., Akkerman & Bakker, 2011) offer a unique
framework for studies of a policy innovation's implementation journey and
complement social ecological theory that informed this study by focusing
attention on relationships of systems with each other. Three major boundary
crossings occur during this journey: (1) from a state education department to
district central offices; (2) from a district central office to constituent schools;
and (3) from a school-wide initiative to teacher-established boundaries in and
surrounding their classrooms.

Figure 8.1 provides a simple depiction of this implementation journey.
Every organizational boundary has associated with it potent combinations of
people, organizations, existing policies, and places (Honig, 2006), and these
variable combinations conspire against automatic, top-down, one-way policy
transfers-as-implementation fidelity. At every boundary, these potent combinations produce multidirectional effects (i.e., top-down, bottom-up, outside-
in, and inside-out) (Datnow, 2006).

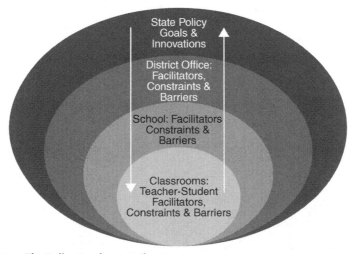

Figure 8.1.   The Policy Implementation Journey

The following discussion of each of these crossings enables a fresh examination of findings presented in previous chapters. For example, it highlights how individuals, groups, and teams at every boundary make meaning of an innovation, evaluate its comparative advantages in their home organizational contexts, and decide on an implementation strategy.

District Central Office Boundaries

The first stopover in the policy innovation journey is the district central office. At this juncture, superintendents and other district leaders enjoy several significant choices as they make sense of policy innovations (Coburn & Russell, 2008). As a part of their sense making, they actively co-construct innovation-ready processes and practices. Their prior experiences, beliefs, and values influence their perceptions of any new policy innovation's features, ultimately influencing the implementation strategy they select.

Daly and Finnigan (2016) describe such a process as follows:

> Implicit theories as to how the world "works" play an important part in the judgments and interpretations that are made as the work of change takes place. The actors' intuitive "screens" filter new experiences and knowledge and thus guide and drive action, while also providing a vantage point from which new ideas and activities are interpreted and enacted (p. 233).

Guided in part by their implicit theories, district leaders have two main options. Both are influenced by the innovation implementation strategies chosen by state education department officials.

In the first scenario, state officials have permitted educators little or no discretion, which may prompt district leaders to act like obedient soldiers. In turn, they may charge principals with faithful implementation in their respective schools, perhaps providing a centralized, scripted implementation timetable. District leaders who opt for this approach accept many assumptions, the most important of which is that the local context is inconsequential to the innovation implementation process. Two other assumptions follow suit: One-size-fits-all schools, and strict district office-school-classroom alignment will yield desirable outcomes.

Alternatively, state officials may authorize local adaptations. In this scenario, district leaders can decide to alter the innovations, change the pace of implementation, or both. Leaders who take this approach assume that the local context matters (Bryk, Gomez, Grunow, & LeMahieu, 2015; Johnson, Marietta, Higgins, Mapp, & Grossman, 2015; Daly & Finnigan, 2016), and so they look for key indicators of innovation readiness and capacity within their own systems (Honig, 2006; Weiner, 2009).

They may proceed with a systems framework (Senge et al., 2012), together with a key principle from improvement science—see the system that produces the outcomes (Bryk et al., 2015). Moreover, exemplary district leaders are concerned that improvement strategies already underway in their respective districts and constituent schools do not clash with the state's latest policy mandates. Such district leaders tend to be protective of all that they have established (Datnow, 2006; Daly & Finnigan, 2016; Honig, 2006), and so they act as innovation-related gatekeepers, brokers, filters, and buffers.

All in all, these leaders tend to eschew wholesale, scripted, and compliance-oriented implementation. Instead they look for the suitability of fit between locally initiated innovations and the state's latest mandates, oftentimes targeting the valuable combination of organizational alignments and workforce clarity and coherence (Fullan & Quinn, 2016; Honig & Hatch, 2004). At the same time, they may buffer their workforces from what they view as excessive innovation implementation demands in an attempt to avoid innovation overload (Hargreaves & Shirley, 2009).

In these ways and others, district central office boundary-crossing dynamics influence a policy innovation's journey. Still other influences are associated with school-level boundaries.

School-Level Boundaries

As policy innovations move to the school level, another boundary must be crossed, and additional opportunities for gatekeeping, filtering, buffering, and brokering arise. Mirroring the orientations and actions of superintendents and other district leaders, protective principals may also act as gatekeepers—if district leaders have given them discretion to do so. Sometimes this discretion is expressed as "distributed leadership" (Spillane, 2013) in service of "accountable autonomy" (Fullan, Rincon-Gallardo, & Hargreaves, 2015) or "defined autonomy" (Marzano & Waters, 2009), as discussed in Chapter 5.

Like district office leaders, principals must make sense of the meaning and practical significance of state policy innovations (Coburn, 2005). Their personal beliefs and thought processes (Spillane, Reiser, & Gomez, 2006) influence their interpretations and actions (Daly & Finnigan, 2016). Their core values affect their decisions regarding what they prioritize, as do the special features of their schools (Day, Gu, & Sammons, 2016).

Principals and their building leadership teams also have to make decisions about whether to proceed with compliance-oriented, strict implementation fidelity versus district-wide adaptations that fit the local context. These pivotal implementation decisions are influenced by how much discretion superintendents grant to principals, and each decision has far-reaching consequences. Two implementation choices are key:

1. Do principals view and treat teachers, instructional coaches, and other professional staff members as implementation puppets, or do they view them as knowledgeable professionals who can be entrusted with adaptations, especially those that align the latest innovations with already established and effective classroom practices and students' needs?
2. Is implementation by teachers in their respective classrooms essentially a short-term event with a clear beginning and firm end, or is the work framed as a continuous improvement project with mechanisms for staff members' individual and organizational learning?

The answers to these questions influence school-level implementation strategies. They also provide an entrée into the school's mechanisms for organizational learning and improvement. Ultimately, the chosen strategies influence whether the policy innovations' journey penetrates the most formidable school boundary: The classroom.

Classroom Boundaries

Chapter 1 provides a look back at the history of school reform, and a similar narrative introduces the significance of the policy innovation journey into classrooms. Countless policy innovations have not penetrated to the classroom to ultimately improve what and how teachers teach and what and how students learn (e.g., Elmore, 2004; Honig, 2006). The CCSS, APPR, and DDI were designed to do exactly that. Consequently, considerable interest resides in whether and how classroom boundaries have been crossed and to what those crossings can be attributed.

Like superintendents at district boundaries and principals at school boundaries, at the classroom boundary teachers must make sense of innovations. Their implicit theories and cognitive processes also influence their meaning making. In addition, all such sense making usually is a collective enterprise involving trusted colleagues, teams of other teachers and support staff, and professional learning communities, and these extend to a school's social networks (Coburn & Stein, 2006).

After teachers weigh the meaning and significance of innovations, they must determine whether or how much they need to adapt them to make them fit for purpose and context. For example, if granted such professional discretion, they must determine whether to engage in wholesale implementation with high levels of fidelity to already-developed programs and resources (e.g., state curriculum modules) or whether to adapt innovations to fit their students' already-developed skills and competencies, typical classroom routines, and favored instructional practices.

The extent to which teachers are treated as professionals to be granted some measure of discretion and input with regard to what is implemented, how fast, and how determines in great measure teachers' motivations and responses to implementing innovations (Weiner, 2009). For example, do principals, instructional coaches, and district leaders elicit teachers' input on their needs for embedded modeling and professional learning and consequently seek tailor-made strategies that respond to their concerns? Or are principals and district leaders intent on providing standardized training premised on a one-size-fits-all implementation strategy?

As teachers decide how to interpret expectations for innovation, evaluate them in relation to past and future practices, and make both permissible and unauthorized implementation decisions at classroom boundaries, far-reaching consequences ensue. Above all, students' academic engagement, learning, and performance are at stake because changes in one part of a system affect others.

These consequences also extend to teachers' resilience (Day & Gu, 2014), their accountability-related work cultures (Fullan et al., 2015), the school's climate (Thapa, Cohen, Guffey, & Higgins-D'Alessandro, 2013) and culture (Schein, 2010), and mechanisms for organizational learning and improvement (Knapp, Copland, Honig, Plecki, & Portin, 2014).

Summarizing the Policy Journey

Framed by the metaphor of a boundary-crossing journey, policy innovation implementation is a context-dependent, complicated undertaking influenced by the potent combination of people, organizations, existing policies, and places (Honig, 2006). It entails organizing and mobilizing educators for collective action, and its success rests on key decisions regarding what needs to get prioritized and done at the boundaries of district office, school, and classrooms.

All decisions regarding policy innovation implementation strategies have a direct bearing on what gets implemented, by whom, how, when, where, and for how long. In fact, what people in local school, district, and community contexts prioritize and do, especially teachers, turns out to be what a particular policy innovation becomes (Smylie & Evans, 2006). What is more, today's innovation implementation strategies and outcomes influence tomorrow's because they become operationalized as organizational readiness and capacity for innovation implementation with continuous improvement mechanisms (Hatch, 2009; Weiner, 2009).

Local contexts—district, school, and community—matter. Although earlier chapters of this book described commonalities and similarities across district offices and schools, contextual variability is the norm, as evidenced in the variety of cases offered in each chapter. This inescapable reality nominates improvement science as a way to monitor and make sense of how and why variability in innovation implementation accounts for different outcomes (Bryk et al., 2015). Comparisons of odds-beating and typically performing schools provided in the previous chapters showcase some of the key differences and help to account for variable outcomes.

CONSIDERING THE ODDS BEATERS AS INNOVATION IMPLEMENTATION EXEMPLARS

If odds beaters are to serve as a collective exemplar, the findings about their practices must be able to answer two questions: (1) Mindful of differences among them, is it possible to derive an overall innovation implementation strategy? (2) What features do odds beaters have in common that make them ready and able to implement innovations without performance declines? This second question joins school effectiveness research with policy implementation research.

An Overall Implementation Strategy

As described particularly in Chapter 4 and 5, leaders in a variety of positions in odds-beating district offices and schools facilitated the cross-boundary journeys of the CCSS, APPR, and DDI. Figure 8.2 presents a hybrid framework that connects often-separate phenomena, namely, district office and school leaders' implementation strategies and teachers' motivations.

The top part of Figure 8.2 highlights three main strategies (Greenhalgh, Robert, MacFarlane, Bate, & Kyriakidou, 2004). At one extreme is top-down, compliance-oriented, and scripted implementation, a "make it happen" strategy, with district leaders and principals in command-and-control positions. At the other extreme is a *laissez faire* approach whereby leaders "let it happen"; that is, they communicate expectations but without providing direct implementation planning, timetables, monitoring, and follow-through.

Neither of these extremes solves the "too tight/too loose" policy implementation dilemma (Fullan, 2006). Each is associated with undesirable and unintended outcomes, both in the here-and-now and extending to long-term effects. A growing, interdisciplinary body of literature recommends the "help it happen" strategy depicted in Figure 8.2, because it encourages "want-to motivations" among teachers and other frontline professionals (e.g., Greenhalgh et al., 2004; Weiner, 2009).

	Make It Happen:	Help It Happen:	Let It Happen:
District Office & School Leaders' Implementation Strategy	Top-down compliance directives with scripted protocols, strict implementation timetable and fidelity standards, tight monitoring, and narrow training.	Implementation entails mutual adaptation, and it is facilitated by responsive technical assistance, social supports, and needed resources, together with organizational learning mechanisms.	Loosely configured implementation plan with variable guidance and monitoring, technical assistance, social supports, and resources.
	Have-to Motives:	**Want-to Motives:**	**Ought-to Motives:**
Teachers' and Other Front-line Professionals' Motivations for Implementation and Performance Adaptation	Front-line professionals feel like implementation puppets, not expert professionals with discretion.	Front-line professionals value the innovation and are committed to adapt, learn, and improve as they implement it.	Front-line professionals feel a sense of obligation, but "their hearts aren't in it," resulting in variable implementation.

Figure 8.2.   Three Policy Innovation Implementation Strategies

This third alternative was manifest in the odds-beating schools and districts. Instead of strict, top-down, compliance-oriented implementation, innovations were adapted as they were implemented, because key people at every boundary were afforded opportunities for input and choices regarding critical criteria such as the meaning and significance of the innovation, how well it fit with current practices, and the pace of implementation.

With plentiful research evidence and successful practice experience to support and justify it, this middle-ground strategy might be called an "innovation implementation sweet spot." It provides an overarching framework for the composite summary of odds beaters' implementation strategies presented next. First, however, three caveats:

- The "Help It Happen" strategy is not a panacea. This "sweet spot" needs to be discovered and even rediscovered as innovation implementation is customized for unique school and district contexts (Johnson et al., 2015).
- The features of schools and district offices as complex organizations matter during periods of disruptive innovation implementation. For example, schools and districts vary with regard to their innovation-specific "absorptive capacities" (Hatch, 2009; Zahra & George, 2002), as discussed in Chapter 5. Absorptive capacity can be thought of as organizational social

capital (Holme & Rangel, 2012), and it takes capacity to build capacity (Hatch, 2009). Typical schools often lack absorptive capacity when innovation implementation is slated to begin.

• This middle-ground strategy hinges on workforce stability, commitments, and competencies, and the caveat comes from several lines of research, each of which has import for the composite summary of the odds-beating schools and districts that follows.

Research has documented, for example, a teacher quality gap involving low-income, culturally and linguistically diverse students (Darling-Hammond, 2010; Goldhaber, Lavery, & Theobald, 2015); the importance of teacher resilience (Day & Gu, 2014); workforce-related innovation readiness, that is, people who have the will, skill, ability, and opportunity to learn new practices (Kane, Owens, Marinell, Thai, & Staiger, 2016); and problems related to high turnover among teachers, principals, superintendents, and other staff members (Holme & Rangel, 2012).

A COMPOSITE SUMMARY OF THE ODDS BEATERS' INNOVATION IMPLEMENTATION STORY

Each of the previous chapters has described how and why policy innovation implementation proceeded in odds-beating schools and district offices, and many of these descriptions were accompanied by explanations. Every chapter emphasizes the importance of the local context, including unique features of the schools and districts as well as their chosen, often self-styled innovation implementation strategies.

Mindful of differences among them, an overall pattern can nevertheless be derived to support the candidacy of the odds beaters as exemplars. To begin with, their dominant strategy conforms to the "Help It Happen" column of Figure 8.2. In other words, leaders at various levels of the system encouraged and rewarded permissible adaptations at the boundaries, facilitating implementation of the innovations. Above all, they encouraged "want-to" motives; this was particularly important among teachers who needed to adapt curricula and modify instruction to become Common Core aligned and culturally responsive.

In short, the odds beaters managed to achieve their respective "implementation sweet spots," albeit not uniformly. The following integrative summary of what educators in odds-beating schools and district offices prioritized and accomplished attests to their status as exemplars.

• District leaders prioritized *district-wide strategies* designed to yield *clarity* regarding the purposes of a particular innovation, its comparative advantages and presumed benefits, and both how and why it needed to become a district-wide and school priority (e.g., DuFour & Fullan, 2013; Rogers, 2003).

- Leaders relied on both existing and newly developed *district-wide and school-specific strategies for crafting relational coherence*, which was manifest in shared purposes and meanings among school and district office professionals (Daly & Finnigan, 2016; Fullan & Quinn, 2016) and facilitated by potent, routine combinations of bottom-up and top-down communications that enabled organizational learning (Honig & Hatch, 2004; Lawson et al., 2017).
- Educators developed *district-wide alignment strategies*, that is, context-specific, operational and structural mechanisms configured to ensure that all schools and the district office were "on the same page" as innovation implementation proceeded; many such strategies included data monitoring and evaluation mechanisms for learning and continuous improvement (DuFour & Fullan, 2013; Johnson et al., 2015; Knapp et al., 2014).
- Innovation implementation-savvy district and school leaders established and supported *distributed leadership structures* such as teams and professional learning communities, giving expression to the idea that adaptive leadership is a function, not just a person's preferred style (Heifetz, Grashow, & Linsky, 2009).
- Designated district office and school-level *boundary spanners* searched their external environments for trends and opportunities, anticipated policy innovation mandates, and cocreated the powerful combination of organizational readiness and workforce competence as they *proactively adopted programs* such as Singapore Math (which facilitated Common Core math implementation) and evaluation tools such as the Danielson Framework (Danielson, 2011), which facilitated implementation of the APPR.
- *Designated district office and school-level boundary crossers* (e.g., assistant superintendents for curriculum and instruction, instructional coaches/ specialists, professional development specialists, and assistant principals), who constituted the often-hidden connective tissue that make alignment and coherence possible, *facilitated top-down and bottom-up organizational learning and improvement* (Coburn & Stein, 2006; Domina, Lewis, Agarwal, & Hanselman, 2015).
- District and school leaders elicited and responded to teachers' expressed needs for responsive, even *tailor-made system-wide professional development supports* because they knew that innovation implementation fundamentally depends on adult learning that is responsive to local needs (Kane et al., 2016; Senge et al., 2012).

- District and school leaders *gained and reallocated resources* as needed (Malen et al., 2015), including corequisite information technologies and data systems for DDI.
- District and school leaders reconfigured work schedules and curriculum revision timetables to provide *shared planning time* for implementation, including provisions for intra- and intergrade *curriculum revision teams* (Coburn & Russell, 2008; Coburn & Stein, 2006).
- District and school leaders regularly *elicited input and feedback from frontline professionals* (e.g., teachers and support staff) in order to monitor and make timely decisions about *the pace of innovation implementation*, adjusting timetables as needed (Meyers, Durlak, & Wandersman, 2012).
- District and school leaders gave teachers considerable *implementation discretion* regarding Common Core standards and the state's prepackaged curriculum modules, creating the conditions for voluntary accountability (Fullan et al., 2015).
- Despite unusual, intense pressure for academic achievement as the sole outcome, and amid all the stresses of innovation implementation, educators in odds beaters maintained *an unrelenting focus on whole-child development* (elementary schools) and *positive youth development* (middle schools), while continuing to focus on *firm connections to families and communities* (Bryk et al., 2009).
- To address students' barriers to attendance, engagement, positive behavior, and learning, schools were implementing special programs such as *social-emotional learning* and *character education* (Smith, 2013), and a few pioneering schools were developing *partnerships with community-based health and social service agencies*.
- Teachers benefited from a variety of configurations and *organizational arrangements for collective learning* and *collaborative implementation supports* such as teams and professional learning communities, which prevented isolation, provided innovation-related social capital supports and resources (Bridwell-Mitchell & Cooc, 2015), and contributed to positive school climates (Thapa et al., 2013) and innovation-conducive, organizational cultures (Schein, 2010).
- Teachers were treated to professional development supports for *data-informed, differentiated, linguistically adapted, and culturally responsive instruction, especially instruction focused on developing habits for self-regulation and higher-order thinking* (Datnow & Hubbard, 2015; Reis, McCoach, Little, Muller, & Kaniskan, 2011).
- Leaders, teachers, and support staff *prioritized crafting engaging and inclusive classroom environments* (Allington, 2010) within *cooperative school climates* wherein all adults took responsibility for the academic success of each child (Thapa et al., 2013).

These innovation implementation strategies serve to explain how and why the odds beaters achieved better-than-predicted results on the state's Common Core assessments and shared histories of better performance prior to the implementation of the innovations, as well. They also set the stage for the companion story on school effectiveness and improvement. Significantly, this second story helps to explain why and how odds beaters were able to proceed with innovation implementation without performance declines.

TENDING THE GARDEN: A COMPOSITE THEORY OF ACTION FOR ODDS-BEATING SCHOOLS

The research team derived an overall theory of action for the odds-beating schools, with the intent of marrying policy innovation implementation research with school effectiveness practice. The process of arriving at this theory of action was neither easy nor linear. This theory derived from multiple phases of data analysis, both inductive and deductive, and it required ongoing team reflection, discussion, and additional literature reviews. Ultimately, it took two years to develop justifiable connections among the forces, factors, and actors identified as most salient to the odds beaters' story. This story is presented next as a composite theory of action.

Introducing a Theory of Action

A theory of action, or a theory of change (e.g., Lawson, Claiborne, Hardiman, & Austin, 2007; Schön & McDonald, 1998), is a pragmatic, cause-and-effect structure that provides direction and guidance regarding what to prioritize and do in order to achieve desirable outcomes. More concretely, it provides a map for a three-phase journey from intent to action to desirable outcomes (McDonald & the Cities and Schools Research Group, 2014).

There are two kinds of action-oriented theories. Empirically based, descriptive-explanatory theories of action, such as the one presented next, are derived from real-world settings. Later, when conditions are ripe, these grounded theories of action can be redirected to become prescriptive frameworks that suggest what might occur in other schools and districts in particular conditions. Under these conditions, the odds beaters in this study collectively become an important exemplar that is instructive to others.

Empirically based theories of action contribute to improvement science (Bryk et al., 2015) by demonstrating one of its central tenets: "See the system that produces the outcomes." In this case, the theory of action maps the odds-beating schools' and districts' systems for producing the better-than-predicted outcomes they achieved during a time of rapid policy innovation.

Piecing Together an Overall Theory of Action

The theory of action presented here has been constructed from the empirical findings that constitute its parts. It is an idealized, composite formation. In other words, no odds-beating district and school had every component, and connections among these components varied from site to site. In the social sciences, such a theory of action is called "an ideal type" (Hearn, 1979).

More than a drawing-board construction, an empirically based theory of action is grounded in observable realities—commonalities and similarities that map across organizations. Salient organizational features involving district offices, schools, and their relationships top the list of these commonalties and similarities. Together they help to explain how and why policy innovations were implemented without performance declines in the odds beaters in this study.

It might be helpful to think of the policy innovations as "transplants" to the organizational gardens of schools and districts. In the odds-beating schools and their districts, leaders shaped and tended these gardens, strategically distributing responsibilities and duties for taking care of the transplants. Of particular importance is the extent to which teachers and other frontline professionals accepted and shared responsibility for establishing and tending those transplants, as well as the extent to which garden conditions were conducive to introducing, nurturing, and sustaining them.

Antecedents for Successful Innovation

Historical trajectories of the odds beaters are important because certain features from the past predict present and future success. Such antecedent features, which include organizational capacity and workforce commitments and competencies, designate essential preconditions for successful innovation adoption and implementation. But schools and districts in the study had these features in advance of the new policies in different measure, developing or strengthening them during the implementation phase.

Whether antecedent or corequisite, the features presented in Figure 8.3 are vital to successful innovation implementation. It is the combination of these features that matters, as well as and particularly how the combination continues into the future. This futuristic orientation builds on the idea that past–present innovation readiness, workforce competency, and organizational capacity help to predict more or less of the same when future innovations are slated for implementation. The whole they comprise is greater than the sum of the parts.

The most important antecedents and corequisites are depicted in Figure 8.3. Some, such as a developmental trajectory of better-than-expected

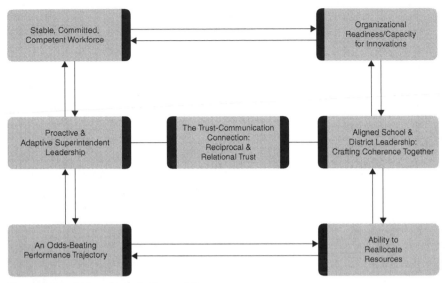

Figure 8.3.   Antecedents & Corequisites

performance, signal prior histories that matter today—and may predict innovation implementation effectiveness with organizational learning and improvement in the future. Others' features are important in the here and now. Some are a bit of both.

Workforce Stability and Competence

All the odds-beating schools in the study enjoyed the services of stable, committed, and educated workforces. State education department databases indicate that compared to typically performing schools in the study sample, odds beaters have a comparatively higher percentage of teachers with advanced coursework beyond the master's degree. Specifically, odds-beating schools have, on average, 40 percent of teachers with advanced graduate-level coursework beyond the minimum required for certification.

Furthermore, interview data show that teachers in odds-beating schools reported being more likely than their peers in typical performers to participate in effective professional development programs, whether inside or outside of the district (Kane et al., 2016).

This potent combination of advanced formal education and effective professional development helps to account for two main findings about odds beaters: In comparison to typical schools, they were positioned better to adopt and implement the CCSS, DDI, and the APPR, and they were able to absorb these innovations without significant declines in their overall school performance. Workforce stability, preparation, quality, competence, and deployment, then, are improvement priorities.

District and School Leadership

The importance of a stable and competent workforce includes district and school leaders. Their proactive and adaptive leadership explains, in part, readiness and capacity for innovation adoption and implementation as well as odds-beating performance. Proactive and adaptive leaders bring to the challenge of adopting new practices knowledge and insight regarding resource-related needs such as sufficient time and structures for collaboration and professional development and reconfigured roles in district offices and schools.

Competent, committed school leaders—principals and others participating in distributed leadership configurations—also are important antecedents and corequisites. Leaders of odds-beating schools and districts are leaders, not merely status-quo-maintaining managers (Durand, Lawson, & Wilcox, 2016). They are structurally aligned as well as professionally connected for mutual learning, knowledge generation, and continuous improvement. As described in more detail in Chapters 2 and 3, they rely on a potent combination of trust and reciprocal communications to facilitate innovation implementation in tandem with continuous improvement (Lawson et al., 2017).

Trust and communication are critical and central to relationships among district and school leaders and other staff of the odds-beating schools (Lawson et al., 2017). This combination is strengthened by leaders' transparency (Wilcox & Angelis, 2011). The vertical relationship between district office leaders and school personnel is cemented and lubricated by reciprocal trust, while school-level relational trust between principals and other educators does double duty as an implementation facilitator and a core school improvement resource (Tschannen-Moran, 2014).

District and School Improvement Drivers

Figure 8.4 presents a summary description of the key drivers for school improvement and innovation implementation as gleaned from this study of odds-beating schools. Some of these drivers have also been described by other researchers. Examples start with leaders who communicate an innovation's comparative advantages (Greenhalgh et al., 2004) and include deliberate efforts and tailored strategies for embedding an innovation in routine practices (Kane et al., 2016).

Perhaps above all, leaders grant teachers considerable discretion to adapt curricula and instruction to meet new requirements and provide responsive professional development. At the same time, they emphasize and allocate resources for the development of the organizational capacities and workforce competencies needed for data-driven decision making and continuous quality improvement (Hatch, 2009).

Another driver is an attitude toward child well-being and youth development that views young people holistically and not merely as students. System-wide, educators in the odds-beating schools emphasize child- and youth-centered priorities and strategies in tandem with academic improvement ones. Most reach into the broader community to forge partnerships with other social service providers to help them meet the needs for social and emotional support for students, especially those at most risk because of poverty or social exclusion due to cultural or linguistic minority status.

Although most of the schools are configured as traditional stand-alone buildings, a few are developing more expansive student support systems. These schools, highlighted in Chapter 7, are developing firm connections to community health and social service providers, augmenting the school's student support professionals (Lawson & van Veen, 2016).

Within the traditional settings, approaches to positive youth development play out differently in elementary and middle schools because strategies for linking whole-child development with academic learning differ between the two levels.

For example, at the middle level, odds-beating schools emphasize positive youth development, social-emotional learning, and character education (see, for example, Durlak, Weissberg, Dymnicki, Taylor, & Schellinger, 2011). Educators extend their efforts to school-sponsored, extracurricular activities

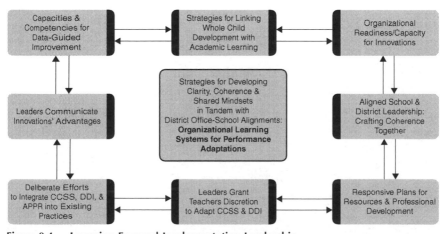

Figure 8.4. Learning-Focused Implementation Leadership

(O'Malley & Amarillas, 2011), participation in which helps to increase both school and academic engagement (Lawson & Lawson, 2013).

All in all, school and district leadership is aligned to craft coherence through a combination of bottom-up and top-down implementation strategies. The drivers shown in Figure 8.4 depict these mechanisms summarized in the middle of the figure. The presence of these several drivers in the odds-beating schools helps to explain why they were able to simultaneously implement the CCSS, new APPR, and DDI without suffering performance declines. This overall configuration also provides an example of leadership for student, staff, and organizational learning in service of continuous improvement (Bryk et al., 2015; Knapp et al., 2014).

Trust and Communications

As discussed before and in Chapters 2 and 3, trust and communications are instrumental in developing a positive school climate. Figure 8.5 presents a framework for school-based, relational trust connected to strong communication networks. This figure indicates how, like the weather's importance for every garden, school climate matters for schools' effectiveness, innovation implementation, and continuous learning and improvement. A positive school climate is conducive to innovation implementation without short-term performance declines (Thapa et al., 2013).

School climate is a multicomponent concept. It starts with relationships among people and extends to safety and security for adults and children alike (Thapa et al., 2013), because it focuses on how people talk to and treat each other. In absence of a positive school climate, professional learning communities, teams, and vibrant school networks are nearly impossible to develop and sustain, and relationships among students as well as relationships with families and communities are suboptimal.

The relationships depicted in Figure 8.5 are fortified when new organizational routines accompany innovation implementation as well as the resources needed to support them (Malen et al., 2015; Spillane, 2013). Shared planning time for teachers is one such resource-intensive routine. Another is improvement-oriented, instructional rounds involving teacher-supported observational frameworks completed by principals and designated coaches who are instructional leaders and seen as such. Yet another is the use of inquiry teams for ongoing review of data to inform instructional and other improvements. Examples of each were evident in the odds beaters.

This mid-level view of odds-beating schools is complete when the box in the lower right of Figure 8.5 is emphasized: District and school leaders of odds-beating schools have developed a clear, adaptable, "Help It Happen" innovation implementation strategy (see Figure 8.2), and the exemplary ones

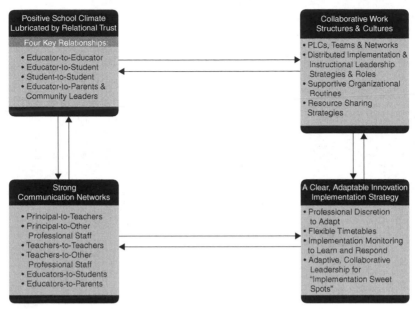

Figure 8.5.   A Framework for Trust and Communications

have done so with teacher leadership and collaboration as a defining feature (see, for example, Coburn & Russell, 2008; Meyers et al., 2012).

Improving the Core Technology

The mere fact that the research team observed instructional shifts in elementary and middle school classrooms at the same time that key informant and focus group interviews provided evidence of the how and why shifts were enacted in particular ways is a path-breaking finding (see also Kane et al., 2016). These shifts, however, remain works in progress because innovation implementation and adaptations in teachers' performances take time and proceed unevenly and variably. They also are in progress as the CCSS are tested in real classroom settings, revealing strengths and weaknesses and needs for revision (Wilcox, Jeffery, & Gardner-Bixler, 2016).

What accounts for the observed shifts in the odds-beating schools' instructional core? Figure 8.6 adds a micro-level layer to this composite theory of action. Its intent is to show how the antecedents, corequisites, and drivers depicted in the previous figures provide a social ecology for performance adaptations (Baard, Rench, & Kozlowski, 2014) that impact each school's core technology.

Because the requisite conditions in the organizational gardens have been established and the innovation implementation strategy has resulted in

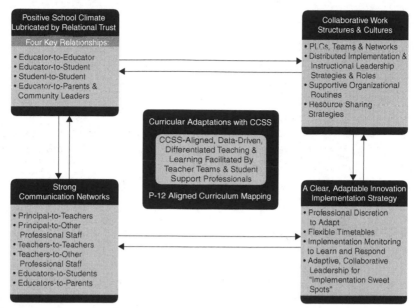

Figure 8.6.   Improving the Core Technology

"want-to" motives, teachers make the shifts in curriculum and instruction. This supportive social ecology is not a naturally occurring phenomenon. It results from the deliberate efforts of district and school leaders as organizational gardeners to skillfully cofacilitate the journeys of policy innovation transplants and for instructional and support staff to adapt their performances accordingly.

Significantly, teachers were neither expected nor required to attempt this progressive implementation-as-adaptation alone. Reflecting Elmore's (2004) warning that isolation is the enemy of improvement, teachers went about this work with the social supports provided by peers, instructional coaches, principals, district office officials, and, in some cases, outside facilitators (Coburn & Russell, 2008).

All organizational leaders are gardeners in this composite theory of action. The idea of leadership as an organizational function and priority (Heifetz et al., 2009) that is distributed widely in district offices and schools (Spillane, 2013) is evident in the odds beaters. This leadership arrangement suggests a learning organization configuration that emphasizes collective responsibility, professional capital, and mechanisms for continuous improvement (Byrk et al., 2015; Fullan et al., 2014; Knapp et al., 2014). It helps to describe and explain innovation implementation effectiveness of odds beaters without significant school performance declines.

SUMMARY

Unlike academic research motivated by investigators' self-interest, this study emanated from a state education department's desire to know to what extent the innovations it had mandated had penetrated to the instructional core, as intended. The mandate had originated with a national policy agenda whose goals are likely to endure. This agenda joins human capital development for the global economy (Becker, 1993) with citizenship preparation (Goodlad, 1994) in pursuit of a grand aim—to prepare young people to graduate from high school "college and career ready."

Nested in this now popular "college and career ready agenda" is another one: educational equity. This other agenda prioritizes the needs of economically disadvantaged students, with due recognition that their P-12 school experiences, in combination with myriad poverty-related challenges, help to explain why many do not seek postsecondary education. Furthermore, too many of those who do do not fare well in community colleges, colleges and universities, and adult career and technical education institutes.

America's promise of equal opportunity—that demography is not destiny (Rothstein, 2004)—is at stake here. Because the odds beaters in this study serve considerable numbers of economically disadvantaged students and are able to innovate and improve without immediate performance declines, they merit the status of exemplars. The practice and policy examples they provide promise to become more important in the near future because:

* Although high school graduation rates have increased steadily over the past decade, the graduation rates of students growing up in poverty have remained stubbornly suboptimal (Civic Enterprises & Everyone Graduates Center, 2016).
* Academic remediation needs for students entering community colleges and four-year colleges and universities in the United States remain high, and low-income students are disproportionately impacted (Complete College America, 2012).
* The fastest-growing segments of the birth to age five population represent low-income, ethnically and linguistically diverse children—the population served least effectively by schools (Annie E. Casey Foundation, 2011).
* Single-parent, poor families are on the rise (Sawhill, 2014), signaling a steady pipeline of young people growing up in poverty who also need educators and schools ready, willing, and able to meet their needs.

These several indicators highlight the odds beaters' potential contributions as exemplars of innovation-ready learning organizations. Their respective contributions pieced together as a collective policy implementation strategy, joined with a composite theory of action for school improvement, present opportunities for countless schools and districts that serve diverse students to become odds beaters. If this book contributes to these important transformations, while helping policy makers and educators at all levels to get better at getting better, it has achieved its primary aim.

REFERENCES

Akkerman, S.F., & Bakker, A. (2011). Boundary crossing and boundary objects. *Review of Educational Research*, 81(2), 132–169. doi: 10.3102/0034654311404435

Allington, R.L. (2010). Recent federal education policy in the United States. In D. Wyse., R. Andrews., & J. Hoffman. (Eds.), *The Routledge International Handbook Series* (pp. 496–507). New York: Routledge.

Annie E. Casey Foundation (2011). *Kids count data book*. Baltimore: Author.

Baard, S.K., Rench, T.A., & Kozlowski, S. (2014). Performance adaptation: A theoretical integration and review. *Journal of Management*, 40(1), 48–99. doi: 10.1177/0149206313488210

Becker, G.S. (1993). *Human capital* (3rd edition). Chicago: University of Chicago Press.

Bridwell-Mitchell, E.N. & Cooc, N. (2016). The ties that bind: How social capital is forged and forfeited in teacher communities. *Educational Researcher*, 45, 7–17. doi:10.3102/0013189x16632191

Bryk, A., Gomez, L., Grunow, A., & LeMahieu, P. (2015). *Learning to improve: How America's schools can get better at getting better.* Cambridge, MA: Harvard Education Press.

Bryk, A., & Schneider, B. (2002). *Trust in schools: A core resource for improvement.* New York: Russell Sage Foundation.

Bryk, A.S., Sebring, P.B., Allensworth, E., Luppescu, S., & Easton, J.Q. (2009). *Organizing schools for improvement: Lessons from Chicago.* Chicago: Chicago University Press.

Civic Enterprises & Everyone Graduates Center (2016). *Building a grad nation.* Data brief: Overview of 2013–14 high school graduation rates. Baltimore, MD: Authors. Downloaded from: http://www.gradnation.org/sites/default/files/18369_Civic_2016_brief_FNL2.pdf

Coburn, C.E. (2005). Shaping teacher sensemaking: School leaders and the enactment of reading policy. *Educational Policy*, 19(3), 476–509. doi:10.1177/0895904805276143

Coburn, C.E., Hill, H.C., & Spillane, J.P. (2016). Alignment and accountability in policy design and implementation The Common Core State Standards and implementation research. *Educational Researcher*, 45(4), 243–251. doi: 10.3102/0013189x16651080

Coburn, C.E., & Penuel, W.R. (2016). Research-practice partnerships in education: Outcomes, dynamics, and open questions. *Educational Researcher*, 45(1), 48–54. doi:10.3102/0013189x16631750

Coburn, C.E., & Russell, J.L. (2008). District policy and teachers' social networks. *Educational Evaluation and Policy Analysis*, 30(3), 203–235. doi: 10.3102/0162373708321829

Coburn, C.E., & Stein, M.K. (2006). Communities of practice theory and the role of teacher professional community in policy implementation. In M. Honig (Ed.), *New directions in educational policy implementation: Confronting complexity* (pp. 25–46). Albany, NY: State University of New York Press.

Complete College America. (2012). *Remediation: Higher education's bridge to nowhere.* Washington, DC: Author. Downloaded from: https://www.insidehighered.com/sites/default/server_files/files/CCA%20Remediation%20ES%20FINAL.pdf

Daly, A.J., & Finnigan, K.S. (2016). The challenge of school and district improvement: Promising directions in district reform. In A.J. Daly & K.S. Finnigan (Eds.), *Thinking and acting systemically: Improving school districts under pressure* (pp. 229–241). Washington, DC: American Educational Research Association.

Danielson, C. (2011). The 2011 teaching evaluation instrument. The Danielson Group. Downloaded from: https://www.danielsongroup.org/books-materials/

Darling-Hammond, L. (2010). *The flat world and education: How America's commitment to equity will determine our future.* NY: Teachers College Press.

Datnow, A. (2006). Connections in the policy chain: The "co-construction" of implementation in comprehensive school reform. In M. Honig (Ed.), *New directions in educational policy implementation: Confronting complexity* (pp. 105–124). Albany, NY: State University of New York Press.

Datnow, A., & Hubbard, L. (2015). Teachers' use of assessment data to inform instruction: Lessons from the past and prospects for the future. *Teachers College Record*, 117(4).

Day, C., & Gu, Q. (2014). *Resilient teachers, resilient schools: Building and sustaining quality in testing times.* New York: Routledge.

Day, C., Gu, Q., & Sammons, P. (2016). The impact of leadership on school outcomes: How successful school leaders use transformational and instructional strategies to make a difference. *Educational Administration Quarterly*, 52(2), 221–258. doi: 10.1177/0013161x15616863

Desimone, L.M. (2008). Whole-school change. In M. Shinn & H. Yoshikawa (Eds.), *Toward positive youth development: Transforming schools and community programs* (pp. 150–169). New York: Oxford University Press.

Domina, T., Lewis, R., Agarwal, P., & Hanselman, P. (2015). Professional sensemakers: Instructional specialists in contemporary schooling. *Educational Researcher*, 44, 359–364. doi:10.3102/0013189x15601644

DuFour, R., & Fullan, M. (2013). *Cultures built to last: Systemic PLCs at work.* Bloomington, IN: Solution Tree Press.

Durand, F.T., Lawson, H.A., & Wilcox, K.C. (2016). The role of proactive and adaptive district leadership in the adoption and implementation of the Common Core

State Standards in elementary schools. *Educational Administration Quarterly*. 52(1), 45–74. doi:10.1177/0013161x15615391

Durlak, J.A., Weissberg, R.P., Dymnicki, A.B., Taylor, R.D., & Schellinger, K. B. (2011). The impact of enhancing students' social and emotional learning: A meta-analysis of school-based universal interventions. *Child Development*, 82(1), 405–432.

Elmore, R.F. (1979). Backward mapping: Implementation research and policy decisions. *Political Science Quarterly*, 94(4), 601–616. doi:10.2307/2149628

Elmore, R.F. (2004). *School reform from the inside out: Policy, practice and performance*. Cambridge, MA: Harvard Education Press.

Fullan, M. (2006). *Turnaround leadership*. San Francisco: Jossey-Bass, Wiley Imprint.

Fullan, M. & Quinn, J. (2016) *Coherence: The right drivers in action for schools, districts and systems*. Thousand Oaks, CA: Corwin.

Fullan, M., Rincon-Gallardo, S., & Hargreaves, A. (2015). Professional capital as accountability. *Education Policy Analysis Archives*, 23(15). Download from http://dx.doi.org/10.14507/epaa.v23.1998

Goldhaber, D., Lavery, L., & Theobald, R. (2015). Uneven playing field? Assessing the teacher quality gap between advantaged and disadvantaged students. *Educational Researcher*, 44(5), 293–307. doi:10.3102/0013189x15592622

Goodlad, J. (1994). *Educational renewal: Better teachers, better schools*. San Francisco: Jossey Bass.

Greenhalgh, S., Robert, G., MacFarlane, F., Bate, P., & Kyriakidou, O. (2004). Diffusion of innovations in service organizations: Systematic review and recommendations. *The Milbank Quarterly*, 82(4), 581–629. doi:10.1111/j.0887-378x.2004.00325.x

Hatch, T. (2009). *Managing to change: How schools can survive (and sometimes thrive) in turbulent times*. New York: Teachers College Press.

Hargreaves, A., & Shirley, D. (2009). The persistence of presentism. *Teachers College Record*, 111(11), 2505–2534.

Hearn, F. (1975). The dialectical uses of ideal-types. *Theory and Society*, 2, 531–561. doi:10.1007/bf00212751

Heifetz, R., Linsky, M., & Grashow, A. (2009). *The practice of adaptive leadership: Tools and tactics for changing your organization and the world*. Cambridge, MA: Harvard Business School Press.

Holme, J.J., & Rangel, V.S. (2012). Putting school reform in its place: Social geography, organizational social capital, and school performance. *American Educational Research Journal*, 49(2), 257–283. doi: 10.3102/0002831211423316

Honig, M.I. (2006). Complexity and policy implementation: Challenges and opportunities in the field. In M. Honig (Ed.), *New directions in educational policy implementation: Confronting complexity* (pp. 1–24). Albany, NY: State University of New York Press.

Honig, M.I., & Hatch, T.C. (2004). Crafting coherence: How schools strategically manage multiple, conflicting demands. *Educational Researcher*, 33(8), 16–30. doi:10.3102/0013189x033008016

Johnson, S.S., Marietta, G., Higgins, M., Mapp, K., & Grossman, A. (2015). *Achieving coherence in district improvement: Managing the relationship between central office and schools*. Cambridge, MA: Harvard Education Press.

Kane, T.J., Owens, A., Marinell, W., Thai, D., & Staiger, D. (2016). *Teaching higher: Educators' perspectives on the Common Core*. Cambridge, MA: Center for Education Policy Research at Harvard University. Downloaded from: http://cepr. harvard.edu/files/cepr/files/teaching-higher-report.pdf

Knapp, M.S., Copland, M.A., Honig, M.I., Plecki, M.L., & Portin, B.S. (2014). *Practicing and supporting learning-focused leadership in schools and districts*. New York: Routledge.

Lawson, H.A. & van Veen, D. (2016). *Developing community schools, community learning centers, extended-service, and multi-service schools: International exemplars for practice, policy, and research*. The Hague, NL: Springer International.

Lawson, M.A., & Lawson, H.A. (2013). New conceptual frameworks for student engagement research, policy, and practice. *Review of Educational Research*, 83(3), 432–479. doi:10.3102/0034654313480891

Lawson, H.A., Durand, F.T., Wilcox, K.C., Gregory, K., Schiller, K.S., & Zuckerman, S. (2017). The role of district and school leaders' trust and communications in the simultaneous implementation of innovative policies. *Journal of School Leadership*, 27(1).

Lawson, H., Claiborne, N., Hardiman, E., & Austin, S. (2007). Deriving theories of change from successful community development partnerships for youths: Implications for school improvement. *American Journal of Education*, 114 (November), 1–40. doi:10.1086/520690

Malen, B., Rice, J., Matlach, L., Bowsher, A., Hoyer, K., & Hyde, L. (2015). Developing organizational capacity for implementing complex education reform initiatives: Insights from a multiyear study of a teacher incentive fund program. *Educational AdministrationQuarterly*, 51(1), 133–176. DOI: 10.1177/0013161X14522482

Marzano, R.J. & Waters, T. (2009) *District leadership that works: Striking the right balance*. Bloomington, IN: Solution Tree.

Marzano, R.J., Waters, T., & McNulty, B.A. (2005). *School leadership that works: From research to results*. Alexandria, VA: ASCD and McRel.

McDonald, J. P. & the Cities and Schools Research Group. (2014). *American school reform: What works, what fails, and why*. Chicago: University of Chicago Press.

Meyers, D.C., Durlak, J., & Wandersman, A. (2012). The quality implementation framework: A synthesis of critical steps in the implementation process. *American Journal of Community Psychology*, 50(3–4), 481–96. doi: 10.1007/s10464-012-9522-x

Neumerski, C.M. (2013). Rethinking instructional leadership, a review: What do we know about principal, teacher, and coach instructional leadership, and where should we go from here? *Educational Administration Quarterly*, 49(2), 310–347. doi:10.1177/0013161x12456700

O'Malley, M.D. & Amarillas, A. (2011). *What works brief #4: School connectedness.* San Francisco: WestEd. Downloaded from: http://californias3.wested.org/tools/1.

Partnership for 21st Century Skills (2004). *Partnership for 21st century skills, education and competitiveness: A resource and policy guide.* Tucson, AZ: Author

Reis, S.M., McCoach, D.B., Little, C.A., Muller, L.M., & Kaniskan, R.B. (2011). The effects of differentiated instruction and enrichment pedagogy on reading achievement in five elementary schools. *American Educational Research Journal,* 48(2), 462–501. doi:10.3102/0002831210382891

Rogers, E. (2003). *Diffusion of innovations* (5th ed.). New York: The Free Press.

Rothstein, R. (2004). *Class and schools: Using social, economic and educational reform to close the black-white achievement gap.* Washington, DC: Economic Policy Institute.

Sawhill, I.V. (2014). *Generation unbound: Drifting into sex and parenthood without marriage.* Washington, DC: Brookings Institution Press.

Schein, E.H. (2010). *Organizational culture and leadership.* 4th Edition. San Francisco: Jossey-Bass.

Schön, D., & McDonald, J. (1998). *Doing what you mean to do in school reform: Theory of action in the Annenberg challenge.* Providence, RI: Brown University.

Senge, P., Cambron-McCabe, N., Lucas, T., Smith, B., Dutton, J., & Kleiner, A. (2012). *Schools that learn* (2nd Edition). New York: Crown Business.

Simmons, J. (2006). *Breaking through: Transforming urban school districts.* New York: Teachers College Press.

Smith, B.H. (2013). School-based character education in the United States. *Childhood Education,* 89(6), 350–355. doi:10.1080/00094056.2013.850921

Smylie, M., & Evans, A. (2006). Social capital and the problem of implementation. In M. Honig (Ed.), *New directions in educational policy implementation: Confronting complexity* (pp. 187–208). Albany, NY: State University of New York Press.

Spillane, J. P. (2013). The practice of leading and managing teaching in educational organizations. In OECD (Ed.), *Leadership for 21st century learning* (pp. 59–82). Paris: OECD.

Spillane, J., Reiser, B., & Gomez, L. (2006). Policy implementation and cognition: The role of human, social, and distributed cognition in framing policy implementation. In M. Honig (Ed.), *New directions in educational policy implementation: Confronting complexity* (pp. 47–64). Albany, NY: State University of New York Press.

Thapa, A. Cohen, J., Guffey, S., & Higgins-D'Alessandro, A. (2013). A review of the school climate research. *Review of Educational Research,* on-line first. doi: 10.3102/0034654313483907

Tschannen-Moran, M. (2014). *Trust matters: Leadership for successful schools* (2nd ed.). San Francisco: Jossey-Bass.

Weiner, B.J. (2009). A theory of organizational readiness for change. *Implementation Science,* 4: 67. Open Access, Published 19 October 2009.

Wilcox, K.C., & Angelis, J.I. (2011). *Best practices from high-performing high schools: How successful schools help students stay in school and thrive.* New York: Teachers College Press.

Wilcox, K.C., Jeffery, J., & Gardner-Bixler, A. (2016). Writing to the Common Core: Teachers' responses to changes in standards and assessments for writing in elementary schools. *Reading & Writing, 29(5)*, 903–928. doi:10.1007/s11145-015-9588-6

Zahra, S.A., & George, G. (2002). Absorptive capacity: A review, reconceptualization, and extension. *Academy of Management Review*, 27(2), 185–223. doi:10.2307/4134351

Chapter Nine

The Sample and the Schools

Kathryn Schiller and Janet Ives Angelis

The schools in this multiple case study were purposively sampled based on their students' performance on the 2013 state assessments, which were the first to be aligned with the Common Core State Standards (Schiller, Durand, Wilcox, & Lawson, 2014). The sampling procedure identified two sets of schools—one called "odds-beaters" and the other called "typical performers"—which were classified based on how their students performed on the assessments relative to schools serving similar populations throughout the state.

This Appendix includes, first, an overview of the method used to select the sample, followed by a short description of each of the schools in the sample, both odds-beaters and typical performers, as well as basic demographic data about the schools.

SAMPLING METHODOLOGY

The first stage of the selection process was to estimate schools' expected average scores by regressing results for each subject—mathematics or English language arts (ELA) —for each grade from third through eighth on the percentage of students classified by the state as economically disadvantaged and the percentage of English language learners (ELLs).

As shown in Figure 9.1, the relationship between schools' average test scores and percentage of economically disadvantaged students was consistent across grade levels and subjects. The line indicates the expected average score for schools with a given rate of economically disadvantaged students. The downward facing "s-curve" indicates that schools with greater percentages of economically disadvantaged students tended to have lower average scores on the state assessments. Thus, the highest-performing schools in the state tended to be those serving the most economically advantaged populations.

However, the cloud of dots (each a school) around the line also indicates that some schools serving more economically disadvantaged students had performance results that equaled or exceeded that of more advantaged schools. The distance between the line and a dot is the "actual-expected gap" in average scores for that school.

At the second stage of the selection process, differences between actual and expected average scores were compared. Two criteria were used to evaluate these actual-expected score gaps: (1) the number of gaps that were statistically significant (determined using one-sample t-tests with p value $< .05$) to take into account margins of error for schools' mean scores and (2) the cumulative size of the actual-expected differences (determined using average z-scores across six comparisons) to consider how large the gaps were relative to those of other schools statewide.

As described in Chapters 1–8, two sets of schools were identified: *odds-beaters,* or those with large and statistically significant gaps between actual and expected scores, and *typical performers,* those whose actual-expected gaps were essentially indistinguishable from zero. Figure 9.1 also illustrates

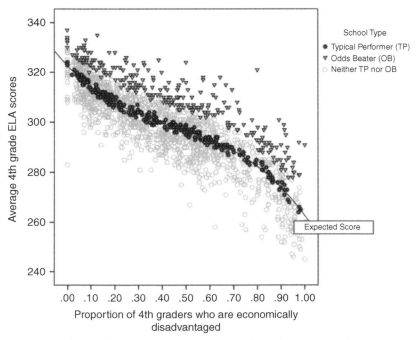

Figure 9.1.   Relationship between Assessment Results and Economic Disadvantage

the difference between these two types of schools, with odds-beaters indicated by triangles along the top part of the cloud and typical performers by the black dots clustered along the "expected" line. (See Tables 9.1 and 9.2 for more on the demographics of each school.)

Schools targeted for participation in this study were purposively sampled from these two groups to be geographically diverse yet similar in the extent to which they serve economically disadvantaged and ethnically diverse populations. While participating schools differed in their relative student performance, all were meeting state adequately yearly progress (AYP) benchmarks and were considered "in good standing." The geographically diverse sample was evenly divided between elementary and middle schools.

In the twelve odds-beating schools, average student performance across multiple grade levels and subjects significantly exceeded that expected of schools serving similar demographic populations across the state. In the six typical performers, students' scores, on average, were indistinguishable from what would be expected for schools serving similar populations.

SCHOOL DESCRIPTIONS

Elementary Schools

The elementary school sample was selected based on student performance on ELA and mathematics assessments for third through fifth grades. The following descriptions provide a sketch of the significant features of each of the elementary schools studied, the odds-beating schools followed by the typically performing schools. For details about each school's demographics, including approximate per-pupil expenditures, see Table 9.1.

The Odds-Beating Elementary Schools

Bay City. The 500 plus students attending Bay City Elementary School can anticipate being greeted by their teachers each morning as they approach the door to their school. The faculty make it a point to welcome students in this way; they said that doing so gives them a chance to see if any students are having a rough start to their day. Other practices at this urban school reflect the school and district mission of catering to not only children's individual academic needs, but also their social and emotional needs, all in an effort to support educational success.

Just as instruction for students is differentiated, so, too, professional development is moving toward differentiation depending on teacher, department, or building need through the use of instructional coaches and the principal as an instructional leader.

Both children and adults were said to benefit from working in a safe, caring, and collaborative environment. Although nearly 100 percent of students in this K-6 school qualify for free or reduced-price lunch, in 2013 the school's performance on the state's ELA and mathematics assessments was nearly 1.8 standard deviations higher than other schools in the state with similar student populations.

Eagle Bluff. In a small rural community, about 400 PK-6 students attend Eagle Bluff Elementary School. Eagle Bluff student performance on the 2013 state ELA and mathematics assessments was one standard deviation higher than schools from across the state, and in 2012, at least two-thirds of students in grades three through five had scored at the proficient or excellent level on those assessments.

During arrival each day, students of all ages stream through the principal's open door, having their shoes tied and receiving hugs and words of encouragement, reflecting both a caring culture and a leader committed to building relationships with everyone in the school. Nearly all of the student body is white, and about half of the students qualify for either free or reduced-price lunch.

Eagle Bluff houses the special education programs for the district's three elementary schools as well as a regional special education classroom. Overall, the staff tries to make learning fun, and they do so within a caring, student-centered school culture that emphasizes mutual respect and collaboration.

Goliad. Goliad serves well over 500 K-6 students in an ethnically, linguistically, and socioeconomically diverse urban school district. The school is characterized by a climate of caring and collaboration, a strong work ethic among staff and students, and a commitment to create a safe environment for children to grow academically, physically, and emotionally with the support of school staff and their families.

Goliad students performed well on state assessments in 2011 and 2012, and the school was identified by the state as closing performance gaps between subgroups of students between 2010–11 and 2011–12. In 2013, the difference between expected and actual average performance on the 2013 state ELA and mathematics assessments was over one standard deviation higher than that of other schools around the state. This academic success has been achieved despite a relatively high rate (70%) of economic disadvantage and a diverse student population, including nearly 100 English language learners.

Spring Creek. Like many schools in rural areas, Spring Creek is situated on the same campus as the district's other schools as well as the district's transportation and maintenance facility. Approximately 500 K-6 students attend this school.

The student-centered focus of the school is reflected in several ways: For example, all students are identified on a plaque in the main entrance way, and the adults in the school make it a point to say that they know and care about every child; they express genuine interest in their academic learning, overall school success, and social and emotional development. To that end, instruction is individualized and an innovative schedule supports flexible student grouping and regrouping.

Teacher turnover is very low, with some teachers reporting that they have taught two generations of the same families in this small town with dispersed businesses and services. Identified by the state as having closed achievement gaps between subgroups of students between 2010–11 and 2011–12, the school also performed better than predicted by its better than 50 percent free and reduced-price lunch rate on the 2013 state ELA and mathematics assessments. Spring Creek student performance was at least one standard deviation higher on those assessments than schools from across the state.

Starling Springs. One of multiple elementary schools in a community hosting several colleges as well as high-technology industries, Starling Springs is a close-knit, neighborhood school serving a diverse population. Its students speak a wide variety of languages and have roots in cultures throughout the world. Educators there credit the success of Starling Springs partly to the outstanding support it receives from parents, many of whom are associated with nearby college communities.

In keeping with the fluctuating nature of engagement in those institutions, a large percentage of Starling Springs' students enter and/or leave during each school year. School staff members have created a culture that quickly welcomes and engages new students and parents, while valuing the unique background each family brings.

Serving approximately 350 K-5 students, with about a third classified as economically disadvantaged, Starling Springs has experienced uncommon student success in state assessments. For example, in 2013, the percentages of students achieving proficiency in ELA and mathematics in grades 3, 4, and 5 were more than double the percentages statewide. In addition to parental support and leveraging student diversity to promote learning, educators attribute their success to engaging and empowering students and their ability to integrate new initiatives into their established culture

Yellow Valley. In the face of insufficient funding and low family involvement, educators at suburban Yellow Valley serve approximately 450 K-5

students, three-quarters of whom are eligible for free or reduced-price lunch. Family mobility is high and this, teachers say, affects students' academic performance. The school is somewhat culturally diverse, with about two-thirds white and one-third other ethnicities, with some of these students identified as English language learners.

Despite these challenges, Yellow Valley students exceeded expected performance on the 2013 state ELA and mathematics assessments by nearly two standard deviations. The school had also consistently outperformed similar schools on earlier state assessments and has closed achievement gaps. Educators at Yellow Valley attest that the school environment is cooperative, caring, and open minded. Many educators there expressed a fierce love for children and strong dedication to developing students into responsible, self-directed, involved, and life-long learners.

In addition to setting high academic goals, Yellow Valley educators also stress students' moral and emotional development, teaching students self-regulation. Their aim is to provide children a safe, warm, healthy, and family-like place for learning.

The Typically Performing Elementary Schools

Paige City. A PK-5 school of somewhat under 500 students, Paige City Elementary School is situated in a suburb of a large urban area. The school sits on a quiet suburban street lined with houses and sidewalks, and the building is connected to the middle school that serves the same area. The district is undergoing a redistricting effort that includes changing boundary lines for elementary schools, teachers shifting buildings, and some building closures. Additionally, student demographics are rapidly changing. Although the rate of turnover among students is high, among faculty it is not.

The district is responsive to state mandates; for example, in 2013–14 Paige City educators were in the beginning stages of implementing the Common Core Standards. Performance of Paige City grade 4–6 students on the 2013 Common Core-aligned assessments was on average less than a quarter of a standard deviation away from the mean difference for all schools in the state, and the school had earned the status of "in good academic standing" on the prior two rounds of state assessments.

Teachers were divided in their assessments of the Standards; with some saying the Standards did not represent a major change for them. Opinions about the new state-mandated Annual Professional Performance Review were less divided, however, with a great deal of frustration expressed about the process and the scoring.

Sun Hollow. Small, suburban Sun Hollow Elementary School (fewer than 380 students) shares a building with the junior/senior high school and the district office. With limited resources, the central administration is lean, and many administrators share responsibilities at both building and district levels. Almost all students are white, and about a third are eligible for free or reduced-price lunch.

In 2013–14, the school was in its second year of Common Core implementation, and on the 2013 Common Core-aligned state assessments, performance fell within .25 standard deviations of the mean. On the prior two rounds of state assessments, the school had made Adequate Yearly Progress (AYP), including for economically disadvantaged students, and was "in good standing."

The district has adopted state-recommended curriculum modules as the core curriculum in both mathematics and English language arts in all grades. Although most teachers were comfortable using the modules to some level, some teachers expressed frustration with feeling unable to adapt modules to meet student needs. They expressed frustration with strict pacing and what they termed the "scripted" nature of the modules and their failure to provide guidance for differentiating for either students ready for more or those who needed more time.

Wolf Creek. Wolf Creek Elementary School is part of a very large rural school district that serves approximately 1,000 students, about half of them at the elementary school. With the other district schools as well as the district office, the school sits on a bucolic campus of sprawling grounds with spacious athletic fields. Its student population is moderately economically disadvantaged, about a third of students; in general, it serves families with neither a lot of poverty nor a lot of wealth. It is also ethnically homogeneous, with almost all of the student population identified as white.

District per-pupil expenditures fall about 20 percent below the state average, and the district was especially hard-hit in the 2008 recession, having cut about 20 percent of teachers. The school attracts several students from outside the district who tuition in. Across the board from classroom to school to district, the staff expressed frustration with the new performance evaluation system and admitted that preoccupation with avoiding low scores was driving decisions about instruction.

Teachers and administrators expressed feeling comfortable with the Common Core Standards and the state-recommended curriculum modules that had been adopted, although there was some conflation of the two— Standards and modules. Teachers generally found the math modules easier to implement than the ELA. The difference between expected and actual average performance on the 2013 Common Core-aligned state assessments was within .16 standard deviations from a gap of zero.

Table 9.1. Participating Elementary Schools

Odds Beating	% Economically Disadvantaged Students	% White Students	Total Enrollment	Per-Pupil Spending
Yellow Valley	>43%	<73%	380–500	<$18.3K
Spring Creek	18–43%	>89%	>500	$18.3–21.4K
Bay City	>43%	<73%	>500	<$18.3K
Eagle Bluff	>43%	>89%	380–500	<$18.3K
Starling Springs	18–43%	<73%	<380	$18.3–21.4K
Goliad	>43%	<73%	>500	>$21.4K
Typically Performing				
Wolf Creek	18–43%	>89%	>500	<$18.3K
Paige City	>43%	73–89%	380–500	<$18.3K
Sun Hollow	18–43%	73–89%	<380	<$18.3K
All Participating Schools				
Median	44%	76%	476	$17K
Mean	53%	68%	501	$18K
Std. Dev.	21%	28%	130	$2.5K
All Elementary Schools in the state				
Median	30%	83%	438	$20K
Mean	33%	75%	458	$20K
Std. Dev.	22%	24%	161	$4.1K

Note: Groupings reflect roughly the top, middle and bottom thirds of the distribution for a given characteristic across the state.

Middle Schools

The middle school sample was selected based on student performance on ELA and mathematics assessments for sixth through eighth grades. The following descriptions provide a sketch of the significant features of each of the middle schools studied, the odds-beating schools followed by the typically performing schools. For details about each school's demographics, including approximate per-pupil expenditures, see Table 9.2.

Odds-Beating Middle Schools

Hutch Hill. Situated on a large campus alongside the suburban district's elementary, intermediate, and high school, Hutch Hill Middle School focuses on positive youth development. Its hallways have been named for various character traits, and bulletin boards display student work, celebrate student achievements, and emphasize character-building traits.

Educators have built an academic and extracurricular program focused on district and related school goals. To meet these goals, leadership is distributed among building leaders, department chairs, and teacher leaders on various committees. The district vision is well communicated to all faculty and staff. Teachers have autonomy in terms of individual instructional approaches, and a sense of mutual respect and support typifies the relationships among administrators, faculty, and staff.

A number of initiatives support students' academic, social, emotional, and developmental needs. These include after-school learning opportunities, community partnerships, teaming structures that include support staff and counselors, and a strong dedication to community and extracurricular involvement. The school prides itself on a history and reputation of success in the region yet does not remain complacent about this achievement. Instead, a culture and climate of high expectations leads to an ambitious pursuit of excellence.

Student performance on Common Core-aligned state assessments in 2013 was statistically significantly higher on three of six comparisons (grades 6–8 ELA and math assessments). In addition, students had performed well on the prior two rounds of state assessments, earning the school "gap-closing" status for closing performance gaps between subgroups of students.

Julesberg. Julesberg Middle School is housed in an elegant building in a busy suburban/urban neighborhood. Inside, student-made posters with anti-bullying messages in various languages decorate the foyer, demonstrating the ethnic and linguistic diversity of Julesberg's population.

The school serves about 1200 students in grades 6–8 as part of a relatively large district that includes several elementary schools and one high school. The school had recently been recognized for closing performance gaps between subgroups of students. On the Common Core-aligned state assessments performance was over one standard deviation higher than that of other schools around the state and statistically significantly higher on three of six comparisons (grades 6–8 ELA and math assessments). This relative academic success was achieved despite moderate rates (about a third) of economic disadvantage and racial/ethnic diversity (about half white).

An embracing and inviting climate, collaborative working model, extra academic support, a focus on educating the "whole child," and support for technology and individualized instruction have enabled the school to implement Common Core initiatives in ways that advance student and educator success. District and school goals are well aligned, and the district has established structures and processes to support teachers and administrators in meeting these goals. Educators in the district also work closely with the larger community and parents to help students achieve.

Laribee. The difference between Laribee Middle School's expected and actual average performance on the 2013 Common Core-aligned state assessments was statistically significantly better than schools serving similar demographic populations (<10% of students from economically disadvantaged families; approximately 85% white) on three of six comparisons (grades 6–8 ELA and math assessments). In addition, the school has a record of good academic performance, having made AYP the two prior years, earning the status of "high performing" because of high student growth rates and the closing of performance gaps between subgroups of students.

The suburban school serves an area that has traditionally been relatively affluent, with mostly owner-occupied housing. However, enrollments are decreasing. Currently, the school houses around 700 students in grades 5–8. A collaborative and collegial atmosphere dominates and was said to extend throughout the school, district, and wider community.

Prior to implementing the Common Core Standards, the district had made curricular adjustments, making dramatic transformations unnecessary as teachers adapted materials to meet the new Standards. Teachers' enthusiasm and drive for professional development are encouraged by the high expectations of parents and administrators. Furthermore, the philosophy of accountability and inclusivity for all students is manifest in the copious opportunities for students to participate in extracurricular activities and the evident concern for students' social and emotional health.

Roaring Gap. Roaring Gap Middle School serves a small rural-fringe community not far from several colleges and universities, whose diverse populations from many countries contribute to the school's diversity. The school population's poverty rate is average for the state (approximately 40%), but the district benefits from a tax base supported by the county's commercial center. This has allowed the school to maintain small class sizes (22–24 students) as well as small caseloads for social workers and counselors, who provide support for social and emotional development.

School goals are developed to address school needs while aligning with district goals, which are developed using student data and input from multiple stakeholders. Structures and processes support teachers and administrators in meeting these goals, such as instructional coaches, embedded professional development, and a coherent approach to setting expectations for student behavior. Building leaders are instructional leaders and are supported by the district in meeting this responsibility.

The difference between expected and actual average performance on the 2013 Common Core-aligned state assessments was over one standard deviation higher than that of other schools and statistically significantly higher on three of six comparisons (grades 6–8 ELA and math assessments). Overall, the features that stand out at Roaring Gap Middle School include: coherence and alignment of district and school goals; distributed instructional leadership; continuous data-driven instructional improvement; embedded professional development aligned with priorities; and intentionally nurturing a positive school climate and culture.

Ruby. Ruby Middle School nestles at the edge of rugged mountain terrain. Surrounded by countryside that was once entirely agricultural, the area had been a blue-collar, industrial town for 150 years, although now only fragments endure. With a declining socioeconomic base and a gradually shrinking population, graduates can no longer anticipate securing a job without some postsecondary education, although vocational training programs, including agriculture, remain strong in the Ruby educational system.

Approximately 75 percent of the class of 2014 entered college. Over 90 percent of the student body is white, and about half of the students qualify for free or reduced-price lunch. The difference between expected and actual average performance on the 2013 Common Core-aligned state assessments was over one standard deviation higher than that of other schools and statistically significantly higher on three of six comparisons (grades 6–8 ELA and math assessments).

Educators at Ruby credit much of the school's success to strong family and community support, with specific thanks given to faith-based groups. The district superintendent noted that school and community have united to weather strong economic crises.

Pre-K through grade 12 classes take place in the same building complex, with approximately 200 students attending the middle school. Features that stand out at the school include: respect and support for teacher autonomy; integrating new initiatives into an established culture of success; solidarity of school and community; and continuous data-driven instructional improvement.

Sage City. Sage City Middle School is the only middle school in a district that attracts families from across the socioeconomic spectrum. Economic diversity (more than half of students qualify for free or reduced-price lunch) is a feature of the school and community. In addition, approximately half the students are linguistically diverse, many coming from Central and South America. School leaders described attempts to meet student needs by providing bilingual instruction in core content areas as well as in art, music, drama, and physical education.

Since the district groups all K-5 students by grade level rather than geography, most students entering the middle school have been together for many years. The school has been particularly purposeful in implementing the Common Core Standards by focusing first on developing understanding of the Standards themselves and then encouraging local adaptation of curriculum and teaching strategies aligned to the Standards.

The difference between expected and actual average performance on the 2013 Common Core-aligned state assessments was close to one standard deviation higher than that of other schools and statistically significantly higher on three of six comparisons (grades 6–8 ELA and math assessments).

A welcoming culture that embraces diversity and age-related developmental stages, team-based professional collaboration to strengthen instruction, a focus on student-centered and personalized learning, emphasis on college and career readiness, and using data to guide instruction and goal setting have enabled the school to implement Common Core initiatives in ways that foster student success.

Typically Performing Middle Schools

Locus Glen. Locus Glen Middle School, housing between 500 and 600 students in grades 6–8, serves a suburban community located in an area near a state university campus. Challenges include an eroded tax base and state aid cuts, budget deficits prompting staffing cut-backs, and families impacted by economic hardships. Budget and staffing cuts have caused elimination of some practices—especially teaming—that supported time for collaborating on aligning curriculum across subjects and for daily discussion of each student.

These cuts coincided with implementation of the Common Core State Standards and new Annual Professional Performance Review processes. Teachers now work to make time to collaborate by checking in with each other and finding ten minutes between superintendent's day meetings to review curriculum alignment across grade levels.

Teachers and administrators are working within a strong academic tradition of excellence and are striving to preserve it despite these challenges. All teachers and school leaders expressed a belief that all children can learn; a desire to work with middle-grade children, and a dedication to developing the whole child. Student performance on the 2013 state assessments was what would be expected of a school serving the same type of population of students. Locus Glen Middle School had also met its AYP goals in either 2010–11 or 2011–12.

Silver City. Silver City Middle School is a large school in a district serving nearly 3500 students. Situated in a community that has changed dramatically over the past twenty years, the district has put a number of programs in place to try to meet the needs of its changing demographics. Educators confront the challenges posed by poverty (over 50% economically disadvantaged) and transience as they strive to educate children from diverse socioeconomic and cultural backgrounds (about 60–40% white–minority).

The difference between expected and actual average performance on the Common Core-aligned 2013 state assessments was within .15 standard deviations from a gap of zero. Additionally, average student performance was not statistically significantly different from expected for grades six through eight.

The school practices positive behavioral interventions, trying to support the social-emotional well-being of students and create a positive environment for everyone. Programs include a college-readiness program that promotes high expectations; it is used across the school, and the approach is compatible with the Common Core Standards. It also has a 1:1 iPad initiative and was in candidate status for the International Baccalaureate Middle Years Program.

The school also focuses on parent involvement, with some teachers willing to do home visits. All in all, Silver City Middle School is a positive, warm, and welcoming environment striving to always move forward and improve student achievement for all students regardless of their backgrounds.

Tarelton. Tarelton Middle School serves a mixed rural community whose major industries are resource extraction and tourism. Local challenges include declining enrollments, resource cut-backs, and economic hardship among its citizens. Of most concern to educators are the challenges of rural poverty's influence on students and the need for additional resources to address those challenges. Limited resources at the school, coupled with limited social service and mental health resources in the town and county, make it difficult. Nevertheless, teachers and administrators appear committed to their students and work to meet their needs despite these limits.

Teachers in particular recognized the importance of developing interpersonal relationships with students in order to engage them in learning, while also providing support for social-emotional growth. In implementing the Common Core Standards, teachers have been given the discretion to use state-recommended curriculum modules or previous curriculum. The result is instructional practices in ELA and mathematics apparently aligned with the Standards, with more traditional (whole group and teacher presentation of information) curriculum and instruction still prevalent in science and social studies classes.

Table 9.2.   Participating Middle Schools

OddsBeating	% Economically Disadvantaged Students	% White Students	Total Enrollment	Per-pupil Spending
Hutch Hill	17–40%	>90%	>770	<$18K
Julesberg	17–40%	<75%	>770	$18–22K
Laribee	<17%	75–90%	770–450	<$18K
Roaring Gap	17–40%	<75%	770–450	$18–22K
Ruby	>40%	>90%	<450	<$18K
Sage City	>40%	<75%	770–450	>$22K
Typically Performing				
Locus Glen	17–40%	>90%	770–450	<$18K
Silver City	>40%	<75%	770–450	$18–22K
Tarelton	>40%	>90%	<450	>$22K
All Participating Schools				
Median	38%	84%	581	$20K
Mean	37%	74%	603	$19K
Std. Dev.	16%	24%	312	$3.4K
All Middle Schools in the State				
Median	27%	85%	620	$20K
Mean	30%	79%	650	$20K
Std. Dev.	20%	20%	317	$4.2K

Note: Groupings reflect roughly the top, middle and bottom thirds of the distribution for a given characteristic across the state.

In brief, the overall pattern is one of selective and uneven adoption and implementation of the Standards. Student performance on the 2013 Common Core-aligned assessments was typical of what would be expected of a school serving the same type of student population.

REFERENCE

Schiller, K., Durand, F., Wilcox, K., & Lawson, H. (2014). *Identification of "odds-beating" and "typically performing" elementary and middle schools: Sampling methodology report.* A report for New York State Education Department as part of the School Improvement Study. Albany, NY: State University of New York.

Index

About the Authors

Kristen Campbell Wilcox is an assistant professor in the Educational Theory and Practice Department of the University at Albany. A former ESL coordinator and ESL and EFL teacher in the United States, Puerto Rico, and Brazil, she was the principal investigator on the studies from which this book grew. In designing the study she drew on her experience as PI and Co-I on a prior series of studies of odds-beating schools as part of the University at Albany School of Education's NYKids project. She brought to this project expertise in systems approaches to school improvement and culturally responsive pedagogies that support diverse learners' success in school. Along with coauthor Angelis she has written two books *Best Practices in Higher-Performing Middle Schools* and *Best Practices in Higher-Performing High Schools*. She has published research findings from this study with coauthors Lawson, Durand, Schiller, and Zuckerman in journals such as *Educational Administration Quarterly* and the *Journal of School Leadership*.

Hal A. Lawson holds a joint appointment in the University at Albany's School of Education and School of Social Welfare and works regularly with colleagues in the School of Public Health. This interdisciplinary configuration reflects his long-standing interests in vulnerable children who need new school designs because they are diverse and reside in challenging places. Two recent books reflect his interests: *Participatory Action Research* and *Developing Community Schools, Community Learning Centers, Extended-Service, and Multi-Service schools: International Exemplars for Practice, Policy, and Research*. His responsibilities on the research team included site visits for data collection, literature reviews, interpretation of the main findings, and helping to derive implications for policy, professional education, practice, and research.

Janet Ives Angelis began her career as a middle and high school teacher. She brought to the research team extensive expertise in the management of complex, sponsored research and development projects that entail site visits to school districts and require tailor-made communications to diverse audiences, particularly practicing educators. For example, she served as Director of Communications for The Regional Laboratory for Educational Improvement of the Northeast and Islands, and she held the same position for The University at Albany's National Research Center on English Learning & Achievement. Drawing on these experiences, on the current project she edited all of the case studies, research reports, and policy briefs. In addition to her service to others, Janet is an accomplished scholar. Her team-based research has appeared in the *Teachers College Record, The Journal of Research in Rural Education,* and *The Middle School Journal.* This is her fourth book, two of which she wrote with lead author Kristen Wilcox.

Francesca T. Durand is an assistant professor in the Department of Educational Leadership in the Esteves School of Education, The Sage Colleges, Albany, NY, where she teaches qualitative and quantitative research methods. Her research explores several dimensions of cradle-to-career system development and leadership. For example, she has studied state-level policy discourses, superintendent and principal leadership for innovation adoption and implementation, and interdisciplinary STEM curriculum development in high schools. She has been a regular presenter at the American Educational Research Association in recent years, and examples of her published work can be found in *Educational Administration Quarterly* and *The Journal of School Leadership.*

Karen M. Gregory completed her PhD in Curriculum and Instruction at the University at Albany in 2014 after garnering over ten years of teaching experience (Spanish, ESL) in four high schools. She is an expert in curriculum and instruction for English language learners. During her doctoral program, she was actively involved in several team-based research and development initiatives to create collaborations between educators of English as a second language (ESL) and the STEM disciplines (science, technology, engineering, and mathematics). Her teaching experiences were invaluable assets in this work. After completing her doctoral degree she became the project manager for the research reported in this book. Her research has been published in *The Canadian Journal of Science, Mathematics and Technology Education, Educational Studies in Mathematics,* and *The Journal of Computers in Mathematics and Science Teaching.*

Kathryn S. Schiller is an associate professor in the Department of Educational Policy & Leadership, an affiliate of the Department of Sociology and the Nelson A. Rockefeller College of Public Affairs & Policy; she is also an associate of the Center for Social and Demographic Analysis. Her research explores the dynamic relationships between individuals and organizations, with particular attention to how school systems structure access to learning opportunities that stratify student outcomes and filter policy initiatives. For example, she was a member of the research team funded by the National Center for Education Statistics and the National Institute of Child Health and Development to identify the factors influencing students' trajectories through the high school mathematics curriculum and their transition to postsecondary education. Her responsibilities on the research team included sampling, survey development and analysis, site visits for data collection, and both quantitative and qualitative data analysis.

Sarah J. Zuckerman is an assistant professor in the College of Education & Human Sciences at the University of Nebraska-Lincoln where she teaches qualitative research methods while advancing her research agenda focused on school leadership, community schools, and cradle-to-career networks. She joined the research team as she was completing her doctoral program in the Department of Educational Policy & Leadership at the University at Albany and subsequently joined Schiller and Durand in a sequel research project focused on the annual professional performance reviews of teachers and principals and the Common Core State Standards. She brought to the team prior experience as a special education teacher in high-needs urban and rural schools as well as expertise in early childhood education.